NOMADS

Peter Carmichael
NOMADS

Collins & Brown

First published in Great Britain in 1991
by Collins & Brown Limited
Mercury House
195 Knightsbridge
London SW7 1RE

A CIP catalogue record for this book
is available from the British Library

ISBN 1 85585 061 3

Conceived, edited and designed by Collins & Brown Limited

Editorial Director **Gabrielle Townsend**

Editor **Sarah Hoggett**

Art Director **Roger Bristow**

Designer **Steven Wooster**

Filmset by Bookworm Typesetting, Manchester

Reproduction by Colourscan, Singapore

Printed and bound in Italy by Graphicom

HALF TITLE
Children of the Hammunat, a Moorish tribe of eastern Mauritania.

TITLE PAGE
Camels silhouetted against the skyline – a reminder of the great
nomadic salt caravans that once plied their trade across the Sahara to
legendary cities such as Timbuktu.

CONTENTS

PREFACE

My preoccupation with nomadic peoples has been part of me for as long as I can remember — a deep attachment that has progressively grown over 25 years of wandering the globe on assignment as a photo-journalist.

It all started with my childhood in Africa. Born in Kenya, I had an exciting, largely undisciplined upbringing on a farm overlooking Nairobi and the game-filled plains that stretched beyond as far as the eye could see. These were wild, carefree days for an impressionable boy who grew up hardly realizing that an outside world even existed. I took the wildlife and exotic nomadic groups on my doorstep almost for granted as a natural extension of my daily life. From an early age I spoke Swahili as well as I spoke English and spent all my time out on the farm in the company of Africans from the diverse tribes who worked for us. From them I learned to recognise the characteristics that separated one from another, the settled highland farmer from the Rift Valley cattle-herder.

Africa gave me so much: a fondness for wide, open spaces from the savannah to the desert; a yearning for adventure; and a lifelong interest in peoples at one with their animals and the lands in which they live. It was in Africa that I discovered what was to become the tool of my trade and my passport to travel — the camera. More importantly, Africa gave me the gift of communication, the ability to cross social boundaries and to live with peoples, nomadic and otherwise, all over the world, from the central Pacific to the Sahara, from the Siberian Arctic to the Himalayas.

I have often been asked what it is that appeals to me about nomads, and I find that there is no simple answer. No one nomadic group is the same as another. There are, however, certain factors that unite them all and separate them from the rest of mankind: their will to move in order to find pasture for their animals; their knowledge of their herds and their environment; a fierce pride in who and what they are. The nomadic pastoralist inhabits a world in which the extremities of life are taken for granted. He still follows the ancient code of conduct that has been passed down from generation to generation: courage, endurance, generosity, hospitality and loyalty. His is a world in which freedom of mobility is cherished and there is an awareness of nature which we, his 'civilized' brothers, have all but lost.

And yet this centuries-old lifestyle is under threat. In many countries, years of drought and increasing desertification mean that the land can no longer sustain the numbers of animals it once could. Elsewhere, traditional nomadic migrations are curtailed by civil war; and international boundaries cut across ancient grazing grounds. Oil pipelines, new roads, hydro-electric plants, dams, fencing, governmental agricultural schemes and wildlife sanctuaries all restrict the nomad who needs space for his herds. Man-made disasters such as Chernobyl, and the claims of an ever-growing sedentary population to land that was once open and uncultivated, confront him at every turn.

Through my work as a photographer, I have had the privilege of living with, and sharing the day-to-day experiences of, nomadic families all over the world. I have gained a great deal from them: an understanding of values very different from those of my own consumer-oriented society; an awareness that their so-called primitive way of life requires a knowledge of land and livestock far deeper than can be achieved through formal education; and a respect for their courage in the face of almost overwhelming adversity. I owe them a profound debt of gratitude. This book, and the four related television films on pastoral nomadic societies, are an attempt to repay that debt — and to introduce the subject of nomadism to the world at large — before it is too late.

Peter Carmichael

RIGHT: A Moorish camel saddle, made of wood and leather.

NOMADS

I N POPULAR PARLANCE, 'nomads' are people without a place to hang their hat. They quite literally have no place they call home. But this definition is not sufficient, as there are many people in the world who live their lives as wanderers but who cannot properly be said to be nomads – hunters-and-gatherers such as the Bushmen of the Kalahari or the Australian Aborigines.

There is, however, one characteristic that distinguishes true nomads from all other peripatetic peoples. The movement of true nomads is not random. They are not simply people who live roving lives. Nomads are people who move in search of pastures. Indeed, our very name for them derives from the Greek word *nemein* or 'roving for pasture'. They are all pastoralists; they are all people whose livelihood depends on the grazing of livestock. Of course, not all pastoralists are nomads (just think of the Welsh sheep farmers or the cowboys of the Old West). The fact that livestock have four legs does not mean that they have to be continually on the move. When certain ecological and technological conditions are met (e.g. fences, stored fodder for winter feeding, artificially improved pastures, adequate stock-to-land ratios), pastoralism is just another kind of farming. But the people described in this book are not farmers. Their distinctive movement unites them in a special category. They are nomadic pastoralists.

Historically, the main areas of nomadic pastoralism have been in central and southwestern Asia, the Middle East, North Africa, and Eurasia south of the Arctic fringe, with smaller nomadic enclaves in Europe, and central and south Africa. Significantly, until the coming of Europeans, there was no nomadic pastoralism in Australia or the Americas. The lack of indigenous animal species suitable for domestication prohibited the development of pastoralism in these areas until the European introduction of livestock. This is not to say that these regions did not have nomads – indeed, the Australian Aborigines are in many ways the archetypal nomadic peoples, wandering from place to place along their songlines – but these nomads did not depend on the movement of domesticated livestock for their livelihood.

The areas inhabited by nomadic pastoralists are widely separated by geography, but they share one important feature: they are all in areas that cannot support settled agriculture. That is, pastoral nomads usually live in areas that are either too dry, or too cold, or too high, or too steep for farming. The mobility of the nomadic pastoralists enables them to exploit the meagre resources of these otherwise marginal lands in a way not possible to settled communities, for once their animals exhaust one pasture, they can simply move on to the next.

Not only are the lands inhabited by nomadic pastoralists 'marginal' in the ecological sense, they are marginal socially and politically as well. Most of the regions where nomadic pastoralists live are on the periphery of settled societies. This contrast is very important. It is often referred to as the difference between roving, nomadic, 'barbarian' predators and settled, agrarian, 'civilized' societies, or, more simply, as the difference between the steppe and the sown. Such a contrast reflects the profound difference in life-style between the two groups, and neatly sums up the tensions between them.

Many commentators take the position that nomads have been pushed to the margins by their more successful farming neighbours, that they have somehow ended up on the margins by default. Certainly, in the twentieth century there are countless examples of nomadic peoples being pushed to the fringe by antipathetic governments and expanding agriculturalists. Yet while contemporary events easily lead to such a conclusion, it may not always have been the case. Current research suggests that rather than being pushed there, nomads originally moved to the margins

The peoples portrayed in this book are typical of the four main areas of nomadism.

● On the fringes of the Sahara the Moors of Mauritania, like their fellow camel herders, the Bedouin of the Arabian peninsula, live in semi-arid desert.

● The cattle-herding Turkana of the barren Rift Valley of northern Kenya represent the southernmost limits of nomadic pastoralism.

● The Mongols, horse nomads and descendants of the great Genghis Khan, inhabit the more temperate climate of the north Asian steppe.

● The reindeer-herding Eveny from the taiga of Siberia – the coldest area in the northern hemisphere – are among the most northern of all nomadic peoples.

by choice. According to this theory, it was the margins that offered them the greatest reward for their labour. There is much circumstantial evidence to support such a position. Certainly in the early days of settled agriculture it was nomads who held the whip hand as it were, enjoying a higher standard of living than did their settled brothers.

Although nomads inhabit huge expanses of the globe, they are dominant in relatively few areas — the Sahara and Sahel in North Africa, the central deserts of the Arabian peninsula, the steppe and taiga lands of Eurasia, the Tibetan plateau. In all these places the pastoral nomads occupy lands where climatic and topographical conditions make settled agriculture impossible. Elsewhere they exist only as isolated pockets exploiting marginal environments alongside settled populations.

The four peoples portrayed in this book each come from one of the main areas of pastoral nomadism and thus illustrate the wide range of ecological conditions encountered by nomads and their adaptations to them.

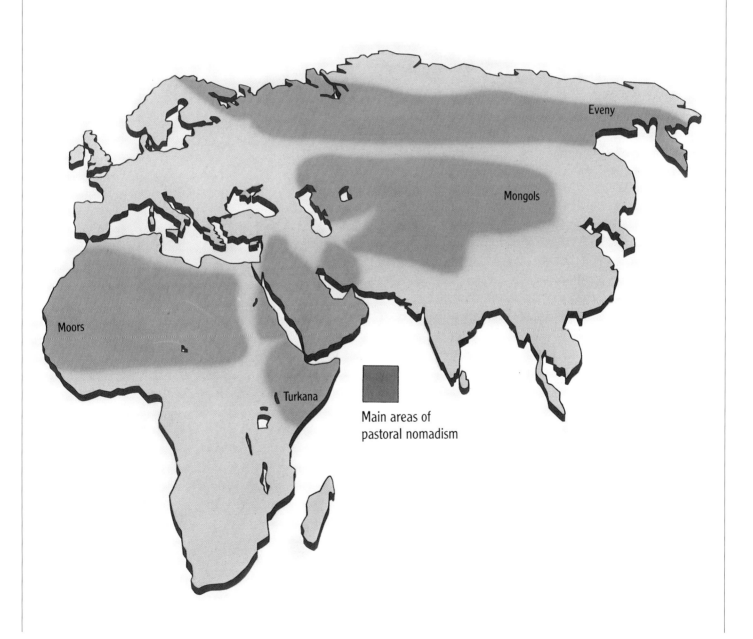

Main areas of
pastoral nomadism

INTRODUCTION

DR ANDRÉ SINGER

> Perpetual movement was their creed, not simply to avert the bad consequences of sitting still, but as an end in itself. In their eyes man was born a migrant, settlement the perversion of degenerates, and cutting the soil to grow crops, murder.
>
> BRUCE CHATWIN **What Am I Doing Here?** (Cape, 1989)

THE NOMAD as the archetype of freedom was a potent image long before Rousseau's 'noble savage'. As an ideal of prelapsarian innocence – Man untainted by the trappings of an acquisitive, settled society – the nomad has long haunted our collective consciousness. Yet the truth is that our image of the nomad is derived from the impressions of transitory visitors to nomadic societies – travellers, merchants, missionaries and administrators – not from accurate research. Our idea of the 'true' Bedouin, for example, owes more to T. E. Lawrence ('of Arabia'), C. M. Doughty's famous book *Travels in Arabia deserta* and various semi-fanciful nineteenth-century accounts than it does to the work of any anthropologist or historian. This romantic image of the chivalrous, hospitable lord of the desert is appealing, but the reality is far more complex. As often as modern research endorses the concept of nomadism being the only feasible way of life in marginal areas, so too does it disclose its impracticalities and difficulties today. Nomads, whether in the deserts of the Middle East, the steppes of Asia, or the scattered brushlands of East Africa, are struggling to survive in a world that increasingly has neither use nor patience for them.

The four groups in this book represent different forms of nomadic pastoralism. The Hammunat camel nomads of Mauritania follow a pattern of movement common to many Bedouin groups and which is one of the main types of migratory movement. The Hammunat follow a pattern of pulsating migration. That is, they move forwards and backwards, often over considerable distances, between wells and pasturelands. This alternating movement is determined by the changing seasons. They move away from the wells and oases in the rainy season and return during the dry.

Across the Middle East different groups cling on to many of the symbols of this form of nomadism. The 'weekend' nomad, equipped with car, television and other urban comforts, who uses his tent and the desert as a way of maintaining some form of nomadic identity, has become a common but distorting image of the form of nomadism that once was so dominant across this vast region. Drought and urban attractions for the young have affected such groups strongly in recent years. Nonetheless, many still maintain the system and style of living of their forebears and demonstrate a continuity that was already old when the Prophet Mohammed swept towards Medina.

One of the other extensive areas of nomadism lies across the grassy plains of central and eastern Africa. Here, pastoral nomads rely upon a greater variety of animal, with cattle predominating, and frequently have far more complex relationships with settled farmers than do their northern Arab neighbours. The Turkana of northwestern Kenya are representative of a kind of nomadism that has come under considerable government pressure to settle.

Many Turkana have settled, but around 200,000 of them still consider themselves nomadic and subsist on the produce of their livestock whilst moving between seasonal grazing areas over which the tribal groups own rights. Although their pattern of movement, form of shelter, type of animal, social structure, religion and environment are very different, both Moors and Turkana maintain the social and economic traditions that they have followed for centuries and with sympathetic support might continue for some time yet.

Traditional Mongol nomadism is similar to that once found among many comparable groups across vast areas of central Asia. The dominant animals were sheep, goats and horses, and the Mongols' pattern of movement, while also determined by the seasons, differs from that of the Moors or the Turkana in a fundamental way. The Mongols migrate between highland summer pastures and lowland winter pastures. Such alternation between altitudes forms the other main type of migratory cycle. Often Mongols would move hundreds of kilometres between their winter and summer pastures. In Inner Mongolia this movement has been severely curtailed by the successive policies of the Chinese government and the Mongols there have had to cope with a generation of dramatic enforced change. With the reversal of some of the most repressive policies in China and Mongolia and the nomads once again being allowed to perform their dramatic sports rituals, the *nadam*, it is fascinating to observe how the symbols of nomadism and those of identity overlap. The limited elements of a nomadic economy that have survived for the Mongols are a sad reflection of the system that spawned one of the world's greatest empires.

The Eveny reindeer herders of Siberia have almost come a full circle. A few years ago, under the criteria of nomadism described above, they could hardly have been classed as nomads. Their homes were in permanent settlements in the village or collective farm, and the herds upon which they depended were controlled by a few individuals. Today, in an era of *perestroika*, the Eveny are attempting once again to move as family households and to reconstitute a nomadic system that had for so long been crushed.

Whatever the individual circumstances of each group, however, there are certain characteristics of nomadism that are common to all the tribes examined here. Nomads, wanderers with herds, do not do so aimlessly, but move with their animals in order to utilize land more suited to pasture than agriculture. Nomadism is a system of complicated balances in which the climate, environment, land ownership and government policy all play their part in determining the size of the nomadic group and the distance over which it can move.

Animals

The question of the origins of nomadism continues to excite researchers from many disciplines. Historians, anthropologists and ecologists are all trying to unravel the problem. There are several theories. One is based on recent archaeological evidence which shows that, contrary to expectations, farming occurred earlier than herding in human history. This turns nineteenth-century theory – which says in evolutionary terms that nomadism is more primitive than farming – on its head. Proponents of this theory say that nomadism is a specialized offshoot from agriculture, one that developed *after* man had already settled down to grow food. In this theory the early cultivators kept just a few domesticated animals. Gradually they increased their herd size, but increased numbers of animals quickly tax the carrying capacity

RIGHT: In the bleak and featureless desert landscape of eastern Mauritania, members of the Hammunat, one of the last groups of year-round nomads in existence, gather around their camp fire.

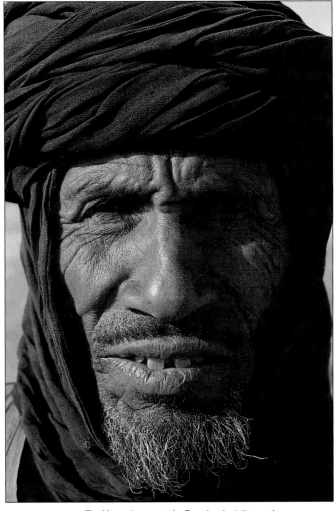

ABOVE: The Moors, known to the French colonialists as the 'blue men' of the desert on account of their indigo clothing, maintain a thousand-year Islamic tradition.

of the local environment, necessitating movement to new pastures. While mixed activities were possible in some locations, herding rapidly came to dominate in areas where it was best able to exploit local conditions and where there was least competition for resources. In this scenario the early cultivator with a few animals was forced to make a choice between staying and growing crops or moving as the animals required. Thus the original shift to full-time herding can be seen as a positive decision; one which gave the herder an increased standard of living when compared with the farmer — at least at Neolithic levels of technology. Proponents of this scenario claim that the nomadic pastoralists that we see today are the descendants of people who abandoned the less productive farming for the more productive herding. That the relative positions of farmers and herders is now reversed in most places around the world owes much to the fact that farming technology (and therefore yields) have continued to improve over the millennia while herding technology has been stagnant.

Animals are far more to nomads than merely a source of food. Their animals provide not only a livelihood but also a passion. In Sudanic Africa, for example, herders' relations with their animals are so close that anthropologists call them 'cattle-complex' people. Clearly, the meat, milk, hide, blood, bones and dung of the animals provide food, clothing, housing and implements for their owners. Less obviously, but ultimately more importantly, their animals also form the focus for ritual, bridewealth, status, relationships and warfare. Livestock pervade the whole social and political fabric of nomadic society. So important are a Nuer's cattle to him, that he will even compose love songs to them. The language of people like the Wodaabe of Niger is rich with terms describing the features of their cows, the shape of the horns, the colour and marking of their hides, their strength, and so on. Wodaabe songs and poems extol the beauty of their animals, and their dances emulate cow movements. The Bedouin even give their camels personal names. The very word for camel (*jamal* in Arabic) comes from the same root as the word for beautiful — *jamil*. The Bedouin can describe an animal by its age, sex or colour. The richness of animal-related vocabulary even extends to special words to describe the size, colour and consistency of the camel's dung! Many thousands of kilometres away in the westernmost province of China, Xinjiang, live some of the last of the Kazakh sheep, horse and yak nomads of Asia. Their attachment to their horses is no less than that of the Wodaabe or Turkana to their cattle. The four possessions, a proverb proclaims, that are most essential for any Kazakh tribesman are, in order of importance, his horse, his gun, his birthplace, and finally, his wife! It is this important and deep-rooted attachment of the nomad to his animals that marks one of the most significant traits that these people share, despite their very different environments and circumstances.

In Arabia, the Sahel, Iran, Pakistan and the semi-deserts of East Africa, the animal best adapted to sustaining a nomadic population is the camel. The domestication of the one-humped camel, the dromedary, began in the second millennium B.C. in the Arabian peninsula, eventually spreading throughout North Africa during Roman times. Today, camel-rearing nomads such as the Baluchis of Pakistan, the Bedouin of Arabia and the Tuareg (or 'Veiled Men') of the Sahara, have much in common. Their camel herds traverse long distances between water holes and oases, along *wadis* or dried river beds, using the marginal grasses along the desert's edge. Camel nomads generally live in areas that could not sustain any permanent settled population and have, consequently, some of the lowest population densities anywhere on the planet. In the Western Sahara, for example, an area equivalent to the whole of Western Europe, live fewer than 500,000 Tuareg. And the Ma'aza Bedouin of Egypt have a density of around one person to every 130 square kilometres over a region the size of Portugal.

The scarcity of water and grazing in regions inhabited by camel nomads has often meant a need to travel very long distances. Tuareg have, in the past, been known to travel as far as 2,750 kilometres in one direction across some of the harshest terrain on Earth. The camel is the only domestic animal able to survive such conditions. In the harsh Saharan summers, camels need to drink water only every five days, whilst in winter, with sufficient pasture, they can survive for months on end without a 'refill' whilst covering stretches of desert at an average of 5–6 kilometres an hour. Besides the camel providing the nomad with his means of transport and wealth, the milk of the camel is one of the most important staples in his diet.

Although camel nomads regard their dromedaries as the most important of their possessions, most of them also herd other animals as a vital part of their economy. It is rare for a nomad to sacrifice any of his valuable camels for meat. Because of the marginal environment in which they live, the most adaptable and hardy animal, supplying more of the nomad's subsistence diet, is the goat. Unlike the doughty camel, the goat cannot survive the long treks across the desert wastes, so most Tuareg nomadism today is restricted to smaller migrations within an 80-kilometre radius, with only a small number of the tribe undertaking the long caravan journeys for the purposes of trade.

Further south, away from the extreme desert environment of the Sahara, rainfall increases and the savannah grasslands can support a greater variety of animal. Camels are often still important, but more as an essential means of transport and less as a focal point for the community. Among many societies in these regions, cattle play an increasingly central role. In southern Niger, for example, the Fulani cattle herders migrate across shorter distances than their Tuareg neighbours and here the cow is the provider of food, clothing and status. In an area that receives most of its rain during one season of the year, the contrast between the activities of summer and winter is considerable. The rainy summer season stretches from June to October, and although it is a joyous time for the Fulani because they can nurture and fatten their beloved cattle, it is also a trying time for they are continuously on the move in order to avoid soggy ground and the illnesses that develop if they remain in one place for too long. Other peoples, like the Turkana, come together for common social activities during the summer months, but for the Fulani, the preferred time for dances, festivities and other communal activities is around the winter water holes. The summer is for exploiting new lush pasturelands. When eventually the rains stop, those plentiful grasslands begin to dry up and are rapidly depleted, forcing the nomads to disperse far afield and begin their migration cycle in search of water holes and fresh grasses. Initially, as the Fulani and their herds move further south, they are able to graze their animals on the stubble from the newly harvested crops. But by the time December arrives, the hot season is with them and both grass and water are scarce and the final stubble exhausted. It is with relief that the nomads sense the beginning of the rains once again and head northwards to complete their annual migration cycle.

RIGHT: The Rift Valley of northern Kenya, semi-arid desert punctuated by dramatic volcanic hills, provides a classic setting for pastoral nomadism. Through an extraordinarily intimate knowledge of their environment the Turkana, cattle herders and hunters, are able to maintain their nomadic way of life despite almost overwhelming pressures.

ABOVE: A Turkana woman wearing the strings of beads beloved of her tribe.

In the more temperate climates of southwest Asia, whilst both camels and cattle might form a small part of the nomad's economy, it is sheep and goats, and sometimes horses, that are the most important. For many of the nomads in Turkey, Iran, Afghanistan, Pakistan and western China, movement is from one altitude to another rather than the more circular movement between water holes or wet and dry pastures. Tribal groups, such as those inhabiting the Zagros mountain range in Iran, move twice a year. In the winter months, the Lurs or Qashqai tribes graze their flocks of sheep and goats in the plains. As the weather gets hotter and the grasslands dry up, the migration begins and the men, women, children and animals journey distances of up to 560 kilometres to reach higher altitudes and cooler pastures in the mountains. There, at over 3,350 metres, they will remain in summer camps until the mountain pastures are depleted and it is time to return to the plains once again. Thousands of kilometres to the east, the horse-rearing Turkic tribes in the Tienshan Mountains follow a similar migration pattern. The beasts of burden here may be the long-haired yak or sometimes the Bactrian camel; but it is the sheep and goats that provide most of the food, and the horse that is the prized possession.

Of the main categories of pastoral nomads, one further group remains. They are perhaps the rarest of all herders of domesticated animals, the reindeer herders of the taiga and tundra regions of Eurasia. Best known of these groups are the Lapps (or Sami) who live in the far north of Scandinavia and on the Kola Peninsula in the Soviet Union. Domesticated herds of reindeer of between 200 and 500 animals sometimes trek distances of up to 300 kilometres from the shelter of the forests in the winter months to fresher pastures towards the coasts in the summer. As with all pastoral nomads, the animals of the Lapps are their primary economic unit. They provide food in the form of meat and milk; they supply the raw materials for production in the form of wool, hides, bone and dung; they are used as a means of transport; they act as a medium of exchange and to some extent replace money; they act as a store of value and an instrument of credit; and finally they can be seen as a means of investment with reproduction providing profitable returns.

Shelter

Type of animal, terrain and climate are factors that determine the form of housing under which the nomad shelters. Clearly, it must be portable; and in many parts of the world it must stand up to harsh and variable climatic changes. To the sedentary population, the tent and sky offer another romantic symbol of nomadic life. The freedom of the sky is seen as an attractive alternative to the mud, brick, wattle and wood that enclose most of us for much of our lives. Yet the damp, smoky, pungent felt *yurts* of the Central Asian nomads, or the dusty, parched goat-hair tents that protect Iranian nomads, or the brush shelters of many cattle herders provide few comforts. Essentially, the nomad's home is practical. Invariably made from animal products or nearby brush, it must be light enough to move from location to location, or easily constructed from materials found at camp sites along the route. The loosely flat-woven goat-hair structures of many South-west Asian, Middle Eastern and North African pastoralists can be easily rolled and packed on the backs of camels, horses or donkeys, and erected in a new location in a matter of minutes. When constructed, they provide welcome shelter from the sun, and are usually placed so that any breeze can circulate through them as a form of natural ventilation. On the other hand, the rays of the sun can penetrate the weave, and during the rare rains, they are not totally waterproof.

In the mountains and steppes of Central Asia, the transportable home is often more elaborate. The Mongols and many of the Turkic tribes who range from Turkey in the West to China in the East have used felt tents or *yurts* for centuries. Even Genghis Khan, the world conqueror, lived in a grand *yurt*. The felt used to cover these conical-shaped homes is made by beating sheep's wool until it is loose and fluffy; then, after dousing it in boiling water, the wool is compressed, rolled and dried to form a thick, waterproof covering which is tied over a wooden-framed dome. An opening at the top of the dome enables the nomad to have his fire inside – essential for cooking but also to provide warmth in the often bitterly cold conditions in the mountains of Asia. Other nomads construct a variation on the theme: the Teda nomads of the Tibetsi live beneath a wooden frame covered with rushes and animal skins similar to the huts, the *aki* and *ekol*, of the Turkana; in Cyrenaica in the summer months, poorer families construct a shrub hut, a *khuss*, around the base of a tree in place of the more coveted tent.

Whether made from hides, hair, felt, or wood, the nomad's shelter is his largest inanimate possession. The other bundles that a Pushtun nomad from Afghanistan, for example, might load upon his camels would consist of bedding, rugs and felts, cooking utensils, pots, water bags and skins for milk and other foods, clothing, lanterns, weapons and some food, such as grain for bread, dried meat and rice. The Pushtun tent, or *kizhdey*, is divided with the bedding and bags at the back, and the cooking area to the front. It is a frugal construct, the only luxury being the quality of a carpet, or today, increasingly, the possession of a radio or cassette player.

The great Asian scholar, Owen Lattimore, was fond of saying that 'the pure nomad is the poor nomad'. His dictum exemplifies the outsider's view of a nomad's possessions compared to those of a settled villager. Real wealth, in all nomadic societies, is measured not by the quantity and quality of possessions but by the numbers and health of the animals.

Relations with Settled Communities

When Adam fled from Eden, and our good world began,
And peasants tilled the valleys – not so did every man,
For Salem was a robber, the first of all his clan,
And he called his sons Salama, Selim and Suleyman.

G. W. MURRAY

In the romantic view, nomads are portrayed either as predators that swoop down on settled communities taking what they want by force or else in an idealized form as somehow free from all encumbrances, representing a kind of absolute freedom and independence. But the predatory or independent nature of the nomad has been greatly exaggerated. Throughout history most nomads have had a symbiotic relationship with settled communities. The key concept here is not 'independence' but 'interdependence'. Even fully nomadic peoples like the Mongols or the Tuareg relied on their settled neighbours for many of the products they could not produce themselves. While nomads did, of course, get luxury items from settled communities (e.g. tea, silk, pottery) we must not ignore the fact that they also got many of the necessities of life (e.g. iron tools and weapons, grain and vegetable foodstuffs) from their settled neighbours. This is not to suggest that the relationship was one-sided.

RIGHT: The steppes of Central Asia, birthplace of the Mongol empire of Genghis Khan, the greatest land empire in the history of mankind, are still home to the Khan's direct descendants. Their culture revolves around their herds of horses, although they also herd cattle, camels, sheep and goats.

ABOVE: The horsemen of Inner Mongolia are now greatly outnumbered by Han (ethnic Chinese). Although the Chinese government is making it increasingly difficult for them to carry on their traditional nomadic way of life, they remain fiercely independent and proud of their heritage.

Settled communities needed products (e.g. wool, horses, meat) that only people on the periphery could provide. This sort of interdependence was common the world over. There is, in fact, no accepted example in the anthropological literature of any nomadic pastoral society that exists solely on the products of its herds. Indeed, nutritionists claim that a diet based exclusively on the products of the herd cannot sustain human life. This is verified anecdotally in the anthropological literature. The Tuareg, for example, a people who epitomize our idea of 'pure nomads', complain of fatigue and stomach pains wherever they have to live exclusively on the products of their herds. Indeed, it comes as something of a surprise to learn that these nomads — who grow no grain of their own — eat almost 200 kilograms of millet per capita each year. This would not be possible without a close and continued relationship with their settled neighbours. Essential goods (grain, vegetables, metal implements, weapons, containers, even wives), all acquired from settled societies, have been a part of nomadic existence since time immemorial.

Most nomadic societies either use their livestock directly to trade with settled villagers and townsfolk in return for essential foodstuffs and other commodities that they are unable to manufacture or gather for themselves; or they use the animal produce to make goods that might similarly be used in exchange. Many nomads are skilled at various crafts and barter their goods in local markets. In central and parts of southwest Asia, for instance, the girls and women weave fine rugs that are in demand far beyond the boundaries of their own area. Many of the most popular rugs found in the plush shops of New York, London or Paris came from the small horizontal looms used in the tents and *yurts* of nomadic tribes, and made from the wool of their sheep.

Pressures on Nomads

With few exceptions, governments regard nomads with suspicion and consider them a source of difficulty and dissent. Nomads pose problems for bureaucrats. They are elusive at census time, evasive when governments attempt to collect taxes, and their presence makes agricultural planning and development in the regions they traverse extremely complex. The education of nomad children poses problems for state and nomad alike, and where military conscription is policy, attempts to include the nomad cause frustrations. Of course, only part of this attitude is based upon practical considerations; the rest stems from deep-seated prejudices and fears. The long history of relationships between settled and nomadic peoples has been punctuated by series of invasions, conquests, destruction and often barbarism from which the nomad has emerged with an almost universal reputation for fighting prowess, ferocity in warfare and rapacity. In many instances this reputation is well-founded. But too often it is forgotten that this foundation is based more in history than in any contemporary behaviour. Yet while a fear of nomadic conquest is today more myth than reality, it nevertheless forms the basis of many governments' relations with their nomadic populations. Contemporary governments feel threatened by nomads. Too often they view their nomads in much the same way that we in Western society regard gypsies — as potential robbers, vagrants, and disrupters of the peace — and, accordingly, take steps to contain, restrain, and repress nomadic activity. Thus, whereas in the past the strength and intrusiveness of the nomad was a threat to the stability of settled societies, today the position has been reversed and it is the nomadic societies that face extinction. Restrictive government pressures, the decline in the quality and availability of grazing land, the attractions of the bright lights of the city and sedentary 'civilization' for the young, cycles of drought and famine, growing controls over the freedom of the nomad to cross international borders, and the extension of 'development' projects (such as hydro-electric schemes, canals and oil pipelines, all of which block traditional migration routes) all threaten nomadic existence.

Nomadic societies are under threat around the world. Nomads' lives are today regulated not by themselves, but by antipathetic, or even hostile, governments with the result that throughout this century they have been herded on to collectives, communes and reservations. Of course, there are exceptions. As Piers Vitebsky shows, in some notable cases the restrictions on nomads have recently been relaxed. Thus *perestroika* in the Soviet Union has resulted in the Eveny returning to their reindeer herding. But in many respects it is too late. Even when government opposition crumbles, nomadic peoples are confronted with the new, and possibly even more relentless, challenge of modernization.

In many parts of the world, this depressing and seemingly inevitable picture is all the more tragic because it is founded on a misconception. Too many governments are unaware of the real benefits that could accure not from the suppression but from the encouragement of nomadism. When properly managed, nomads can usefully exploit marginal lands and play an important part in the economic and social life of any country.

Throughout the descriptions of the four nomadic societies in this book, words such as 'persecution' and 'struggle' are sprinkled liberally alongside the more stereotypic 'freedom', 'space', 'mobility' and 'independence'. In the end, the contradictions are never fully resolved. Yet clear patterns emerge, as does, most importantly of all, a greater understanding of the nomads' relationship to their environment. It is their unique use of land, water and animals that unites these disparate peoples. The life of the camel-herding Moors of Mauritania may soon be inexorably metamorphosed into a more uniform technology-dominated Westernized world. But until that happens, they share with the horse-breeding Mongols of China, the reindeer-raising Eveny of Siberia and the cattle-herding Turkana of Kenya a knowledge and love of their livestock that has enabled them not merely to survive, but to do so in a manner that sustains their traditions, protects a rich social life, maintains a balance with their neighbours, and continues to preserve the land around them for the future. Nomadism has survived and has proven itself to be an efficient use of resources over a very long period. Perhaps these chapters will help to provide an insight into a unique and threatened cultural heritage. It would be a tragedy were this to be merely a record for future generations of a way of life that was viable from prehistoric times, only to be destroyed by the materialism and standardization of the twentieth century.

RIGHT: The rugged mountains of Siberia, the coldest area in the northern hemisphere with winter temperatures falling as low as minus 70 degrees Celsius, are home to the Eveny, reindeer herders whose lives still revolve around their animals' annual migration.

ABOVE: The Eveny, who today number about 17,000, are just one of twenty-six 'small peoples' of Siberia and the Soviet North.

THE
MOORS
OF MAURITANIA

DIANA STONE

The Moors, camel herders on the fringes of the Sahara whose forefathers once plied their trade in such legendary cities as Timbuktu, are one of the largest groups of year-round nomads in the world today. In the barren, featureless desert, they maintain their distinctive culture and a thousand-year Islamic tradition.

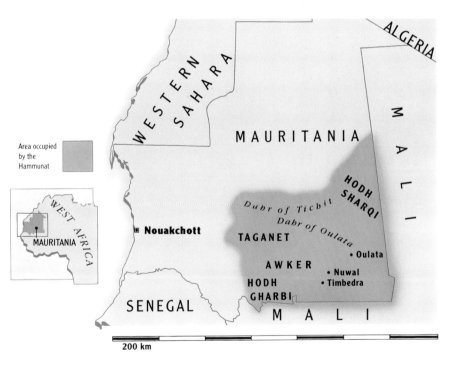

Area occupied by the Hammunat

200 km

LEFT: The Hammunat Moors of eastern Mauritania are camel herders and one of the last groups of year-round nomads in a country that was, until recently, predominantly nomadic.

THE MOORS who call themselves *bidan* 'the white men' are a Muslim people of mixed Arab and Berber origin who live nowadays mostly in the Islamic republic of Mauritania, a vast country twice the size of France, and consisting mostly of desert. The Moors and their former slaves (the *haratin*, who are of African origin and share the Moors' language and culture) make up the majority of Mauritania's population of around two million. In the south of Mauritania along the Senegal river, and in the regions bordering Mali, live a number of Muslim Negro-African groups – the Halpulaar, Soninke, Wolof, Peul and Bambara. With the exception of the Peul, who are cattle nomads, these groups are mainly agriculturalists.

Moors are also found in the Western Sahara, northern Mali, southern Morocco and Algeria. They all speak an Arabic dialect known as Hassaniyya, and shared until recently a nomadic way of life.

The Moors are little known to Westerners today, yet surprisingly Europeans have been in contact with them from at least the eleventh century when the Almoravids swept up through North Africa to conquer southern Spain. The Portuguese, and later the Dutch, British and French, traded with Moors from the fifteenth century onwards; and in the eighteenth and nineteenth centuries the Moors were one of the world's largest suppliers of gum Arabic. However, this trade was confined to the Atlantic coast and ports along the Senegal river and Europeans knew very little about the vast desert interior of Mauritania and its inhabitants. Attempts to chart the region met the opposition of its inhabitants, and travellers were often captured and in some cases even killed. As a result, the Moors were feared and portrayed as difficult and treacherous. It was with great difficulty that the French were able to occupy Mauritania in the early part of the twentieth century, and only in 1934 was the whole country 'pacified' (the expression used by Xavier Coppolani, who planned the French occupation of Mauritania). During the colonial period French accounts of the Moors alternated between portraying them as romantic nomadic 'blue men' (so called because of the way that the indigo dye of their clothing rubbed off on their skin, leaving a bluish tint) living in biblical surroundings, and criticizing them for what the French perceived to be their 'feudal' way of life. In the post-colonial period relatively little work, even by the French, has been done on the Moors with the result that far less is known about them than about their neighbours to the west and north.

Moorish Social Organization

All Moors belong to a particular tribe or *qabila*. The members of each tribe consider themselves to be *awlad amm*, which means paternal cousins, and trace their descent from a common ancestor whose name the tribe often bears. However, as the Moors themselves admit, tribes are often composed of groups of differing origins brought together through political alliances, intermarriage, wars and other factors. There are at least one hundred named tribes in Mauritania.

In the past a hierarchy cut across the tribal system. At the top of the hierarchy were the tribes of warriors and raiders (*Hassan*) who controlled the four emirates established in Mauritania in the seventeenth and eighteenth centuries. Tribes classified as *Zawaya* (religious specialists – Islamic scholars, judges, *imams*, religious teachers, healers, doctors, mystical leaders, saints, miracle workers and so on) also occupied a position of great authority. They owned most of the herds, organized agricultural activities and the caravan trade and were responsible for digging many of the wells. In addition, they helped to spread the Islamic faith throughout West Africa. Next in the hierarchy came the herding specialists (*Zenaga*). Within tribes there were further sub-categories of the hierarchy – artisans, musicians, ex-slaves and slaves.

This hierarchy was never totally rigid. As circumstances changed, people passed from one category to another. The system also differed from one region of Mauritania to another.

LEFT: After being out to pasture during the day, goats (and sheep) are brought back to the camp at night. To prevent them from drinking their mothers' milk, the kids are attached together with a long rope or placed in enclosures made from branches.

During the colonial period the French attempted gradually to dismantle the hierarchical system. In particular, they tried to put an end to the system of paying tribute that was the backbone of the *Hassan* emiral tribes' power and the *Hassan* eventually lost much of their power. Many *Zawaya* tribes, on the other hand, consolidated and extended their power because their religious and trading background allowed them to take advantage of changes precipitated by colonial rule. They were the first, for instance, to take advantage of the colonial education system and the commercial opportunities offered by the introduction of the market economy. This has spilled over into the post-colonial period: although some *Hassan* tribes have considerable power in Mauritania today, a significant number of politicians and entrepreneurs come from a *Zawaya* background. Mauritania is unusual in that it is one of the few states in Africa in which most of the population and successive government leaders are from a nomadic background. One result of this is that, unlike elsewhere, nomads are not perceived as a threatening minority who have to be settled.

At the time of Mauritanian independence in 1960, at least 85 per cent of the Moors were nomadic and no city had a population of more than six thousand. In the last few decades, however, nomads have settled in their thousands. The increasing importance of the market economy during the colonial and post-colonial period created new labour relations and new forms of trade. These changes eroded the Moors' traditional pastoral nomadic economy and way of life and led to migration and settlement. But settlement occurred on an unprecedented scale after the devastating droughts of the late 1960s as people could no longer survive as pastoral nomads. From 85 per cent in 1960, the nomadic population fell to 36 per cent in 1976 and 12 per cent in 1988. People had to search for new ways of making a living. One of the most interesting developments in this respect has been a turn towards agriculture among the Moors who in the past, apart from the slave and *haratin* groups, had no experience as agriculturalists. Although no figures are available on the extent of these new practices, they are fairly widespread as any visit to the new villages that have sprung up throughout Mauritania demonstrates. The building of dams along

ABOVE: Goats are milked at or before dawn and again just after nightfall, and their milk provides a major part of the Hammunat's diet.

RIGHT: Young boys often accompany the sheep and goats to pasture and even very young children help their parents by tethering the young animals at various times of day.

the Senegal river, which has made irrigated agriculture possible on a massive scale, and the change of land laws in 1983, have also contributed to this shift. In spite of the changes in their lifestyle, settled Moors remain extremely attached to, and proud of, their nomadic past and frequently recreate it by pitching tents outside their houses. Those who have the means keep herds that are minded by hired hands, and escape to the desert for weekends and holidays to visit their herds and drink milk.

Most of the nomads in Mauritania today are found in the east of the country known as the Hodh. The sheer distance of the Hodh from both the administrative capital of colonial Mauritania (Saint Louis, Senegal) and Nouakchott, the new capital after independence, to some extent cut off the region from the rest of the country. Until the late 1970s no effective road network linked the Hodh with the capital and it was easier to travel to Bamako, the capital of Mali, than to Nouakchott. The region's relative isolation and its fertile pastures are two reasons why a pastoral nomadic way of life continues to flourish there. This chapter looks at the Hammunat of the Hodh Sharqi, one of the largest groups of camel nomads in Mauritania today.

The Hammunat and their History

Although no figures exist, at a rough estimate the Hammunat, who are divided into twelve named factions, probably number at least 25,000. Around two-thirds of the tribe remain nomadic and move through a vast territory that extends north of Awker into neighbouring Mali.

The Hammunat were part of the Mechdouf tribe, founded around the sixteenth century by two men, Mechdouf and Bu Hommad. Like other tribes of Berber origin in Mauritania, the Mechdouf were gradually 'Arabized', and abandoned their earlier language, as they came into contact with Arab tribes that migrated into the area from the fourteenth century onwards.

By the latter part of the nineteenth century, the Mechdouf had become a vast assembly of tribes and factions of heterogeneous origin and dominated the Hodh. Political power was concentrated in one family, the Ahl M'haimid, who traced their

RIGHT: Hammunat women wear a long piece of cloth known as a *melhafa*, which they drape around their bodies and over their heads (although they do not, unlike women in many other Muslim societies, cover their faces). These are usually indigo in colour. When new the dye tends to come off and stain the women's skin blue; this is believed to protect the skin from the effects of sun and wind, and also to whiten it. The indigo *melhafa* are made from a heavy cotton that offers some protection against the cold. Hammunat women wear nothing underneath except cotton skirts (if they have them). Younger women occasionally wear lighter cotton *melhafa* that come in a variety of designs and colours. These are now worn throughout Mauritania. They are often transparent and have to be worn with dresses or skirts underneath.

LEFT: Hammunat men wear turbans known as *hawli* – long pieces of cotton which are usually white or blue in colour. Some men wear indigo turbans, the dye of which comes off on their faces giving them a bluish tinge. It was for this reason that the French colonialists referred to the Moors as the 'blue men' of the desert.

Preparing for the Move

The Hammunat move frequently in search of water and pasture for their animals. Moves take place early in the morning, when the temperature is still relatively low. The women take down and fold up the tents and, with the help of their husbands and children, load the family's possessions on the backs of their camels.

RIGHT: Camels – the only animals that can move easily over the soft desert sand – are used by the Hammunat as beasts of burden.

TOP: Cooking pots and containers are attached to the side of the *rhal*, a wooden platform with carved legs which is the property of the wife. The *rhal* also serves as a sort of camel saddle, used by the women and young children when the family moves from one location to another.

RIGHT: The tent poles are tied together for transportation. The curved tent poles are made by the Hammunat themselves from the wood of a tree known as tikifit (*Combretum glutinosum*). The longer upright poles are made from a tree known as deambu, which grows in the area near the Malian border. These are usually bought ready-made from artisans.

descent from the original founders of the tribe. However, the Ahl M'haimids' power was extremely fragile and unstable owing to frequent feuds and struggles over succession among the Mechdouf themselves, and constant raiding and wars between the Mechdouf and other Moorish tribes.

At the end of the nineteenth century, the Hammunat constituted an important warrior faction of the Mechdouf and had a relatively autonomous position within the tribe. Their autonomy derived largely from their specialization in camel raising. As camel herders the Hammunat were able to survive as nomads in an area to the north of the majority of the Mechdouf, whose specialization in cattle raising demanded a different environment, and this gave the Hammunat a degree of independence. Camel raising both allows and depends on the ability of small highly mobile groups to move rapidly across vast distances and this capacity for mobility was in turn a prerequisite for successful warriors and raiders. In the past the Hammunat had a formidable reputation as warriors, a memory that is kept alive today through their colloquial poetry and oral history. Finally, by virtue of their occupation of a vast and inaccessible area, the Hammunat attracted large numbers of exiles and emigrants from other tribes, thereby giving them numerical strength within the Mechdouf.

At the end of the nineteenth century, the Hammunat began to split from the Mechdouf. By the time the French had 'pacified' the two Hodhs (which became attached to French Sudan) enough to enter the ancient caravan city of Oulata in 1912, they recognized the Hammunat as a separate tribe. Describing the Moors of the time as existing in a 'state of anarchy', the French attempted to put an end to the wars, assassinations and raiding that were endemic in Moorish society. However, conflicts continued – at least during the early years of colonialism. Raiding, in particular, went on since the tribes of the northern part of Mauritania and the Western Sahara remained free of French control.

One effect of the French colonial period, however, was to fix power definitively in the hands of certain factions and families who acted as intermediaries between their tribe and the French. The French reorganized the Hammunat into twelve factions and recognized the authority of the chief of each one. The authority of these families persists, albeit in a modified form, to this day. The chiefs of the Ahl Lekhal and the Oulad Wafi factions, for instance, are both mayors today.

PREVIOUS PAGE
The tribe on the move. The women and young children ride on camels while the men walk alongside.

BELOW: Setting up the tent. The tent poles are driven into the sand and a heavy cotton covering thrown over them. Some tents have straight poles in the centre with curved ones at the ends; others have only curved poles.

RIGHT: Women and children outside their tents. Many of the women's tasks tend to confine them to the tent and its immediate environs.

The Hammunat today: Camps and Tents

The nomadic Hammunat live in camps called *frig* composed of individual tents. The size of these camps varies depending on the season and the availability of pasture. In the rainy season, when pasture is abundant, camps can consist of as many as twenty tents; but at all other times camps tend to be restricted to no more than five tents. Although camps most often consist of a small family group, they can include the tents of cousins or even members of different tribes linked through marriage alliances, religious links or common economic interests. The spacing of tents in an encampment often reflects the relationships of the members: the tents of a father and his married sons are usually pitched fairly close to one another, with the tents of married daughters and their husbands pitched slightly further away and cousins or strangers to the tribe at the limits of the camp.

It is significant that the word for tent and family – *khayme* – is the same in Hassaniyya, and that one of the terms for marriage is derived from the same root, because individual tents are fabricated and set up as a result of marriage. Hammunat girls tend to marry young, at around twelve or thirteen, with the groom usually in his twenties. The wedding is a drawn-out affair, with a long period of time often

LEFT: A young Hammunat girl pokes at the embers of the camp fire. Hammunat children, like all nomads, take an active part in the day-to-day running of the camp.

RIGHT: A slaughtered goat. Animals are slaughtered according to strict Muslim dietary laws, by slitting their throats and letting the blood run from the body. These laws also forbid the consumption of meat from animals that have died of natural causes, and so an old or sick animal is often slaughtered before it dies. The Hammunat also slaughter sheep and goats when an important guest arrives or at baptisms, weddings or on religious festivals. Apart from these occasions, the Hammunat rarely eat meat (and are often hungry).

separating the religious act, the wedding party, and the time the couple eventually set up a tent together. Marriage also involves a complicated exchange of gifts between the two families, their relatives and friends. The groom has to pay the *sdaq*, which nowadays is paid in cash, to the girl. (In the past, camels were given as payment.) In addition, he gives a chest to the bride filled with clothes, perfumes and other items that she distributes to the women of her camp.

Hammunat weddings are elaborate affairs. Held at the bride's camp and lasting a day and a half, they are a focus for family and friends from far afield. The men have camel races, firing their guns in the air to honour the winner. The bride has her hair plaited and her hands and feet painted with henna. She is not supposed to be seen during the day. At night she is brought out by the friends of the bridegroom (this happens at all traditional Moorish weddings), but is 'stolen' after a ritual fight by her friends and taken away and hidden. The bridegroom's friends have to find her (this can go on for days) and bring her back to him. After a night of singing and dancing, the bride and bridegroom go to a tent that has been set up for them and spend the night there, but the marriage is rarely consummated at this stage.

After the wedding party, the bride continues living with her parents until at least a year after her marriage. She is visited from time to time by her husband and they spend the night together in a small tent set up at the outskirts of the camp. Her husband will give gifts to her family, and her mother will prepare the *fiskha* which is made up of mats, cushions, jewellery, and other decorative objects which the bride will distribute to her in-laws when she goes to live in their camp.

A married couple's first tent is made by the mother of the bride. Although the tent or family is known by the name of the husband and father, the tent itself remains the property of the wife in the case of divorce (which is not uncommon among the Hammunat). Indeed men, who are monogamous in Moorish society, can only live in the tent of their wife (or, if they are single or divorced, in the tent of their parents, sister or other female relative), whereas a woman can live alone.

In the past women wove tents from black goat's hair, but these are now rare — partly because of the cost and labour involved in making them and also because,

LEFT: Very young Hammunat boys either go naked or are dressed in imported European clothes. All circumcized boys (boys are usually circumcized between the ages of six and eleven) wear clothes. The heads of babies, uncircumcized boys, and girls up to the age of about eight are usually partially shaved because, according to the Hammunat, shaving the heads in this way lengthens the children's lives. Again, this is a traditional practice that has virtually died out elsewhere in Mauritania.

RIGHT: A young Hammunat girl swings from the pole of her tent. Girls usually start to wear clothes from the age of six or seven and will begin to wear the *melhafa* before puberty.

according to the Hammunat, they are too heavy and hot. Nowdays tents are made from a heavy cotton known as *jif* which is imported from Mali and sold in strips that Hammunat women then sew together and decorate around the corners with colourful embroidered panels. Tents, which are set up and taken down by women, are always pitched east to west with the front opening to the west. The interior of the tent is also the woman's responsibility. The ground area, which is rectangular and can measure up to 6 metres across, is either left clear or covered with woven mats made by the women from strips of palm and leather, blankets and leather cushions. Women's objects, mostly made by artisans, are always arranged to the north side of the tent and are either placed on, under or attached to the *rhal*, a wooden platform with carved legs. These objects usually include a metal trunk, in which clothes, perfumes and mirrors may be stored, and blankets, bowls, gourds, funnels, cooking pots, milking utensils and animal-skin containers. When the family is on the move, the *rhal* is also used, placed upside down, as a camel saddle for women and children; and the family's possessions are attached to either side. The decorated leather bags known as *tassufra*, in which the men store their firearms, tea utensils and other items, are often placed on the *rhal* and the keys given to their wives as a mark of trust. At night the father sleeps next to the *rhal* with his wife, and the children sleep behind him – apparently to protect the family against disease and attacks from malevolent spirits which, according to the Hammunat, often come from the north.

The men's camel saddles, which are made of leather and wood, are often placed on the south side of the tent or in front. Other possessions that may belong to either men or women, such as the large metal drums used to fetch and store water and the metal bowls that the animals drink from, are also kept in front of the tent.

Many of the domestic and economic activities performed by women tend to confine them to the tent and its immediate environs. Apart from child care, one of the most important of their tasks is to organize meals for the family and guests. The

RIGHT: In the game of *seeg*, which is played by women, sand is scraped into a mound and divided into ridges. It can be played between two women or between teams of several players. One side plays with pieces of animal dung, the other with pieces of cut grass. Pieces of bark are used like dice and are thrown to establish a score that allows the pieces to be moved around the sand ridges. The idea is to get all the pieces home without being taken by the other side. *Seeg* is played with great gusto and the women often encourage each other by shouting and singing.

BELOW: *Dhamit* is played by the men and is set up by tracing a series of lines in the sand. As with *seeg*, the opposing players' 'counters' are either pieces of animal dung or cut grass. The game is like a complex version of draughts and, to be played well, requires a good deal of concentration.

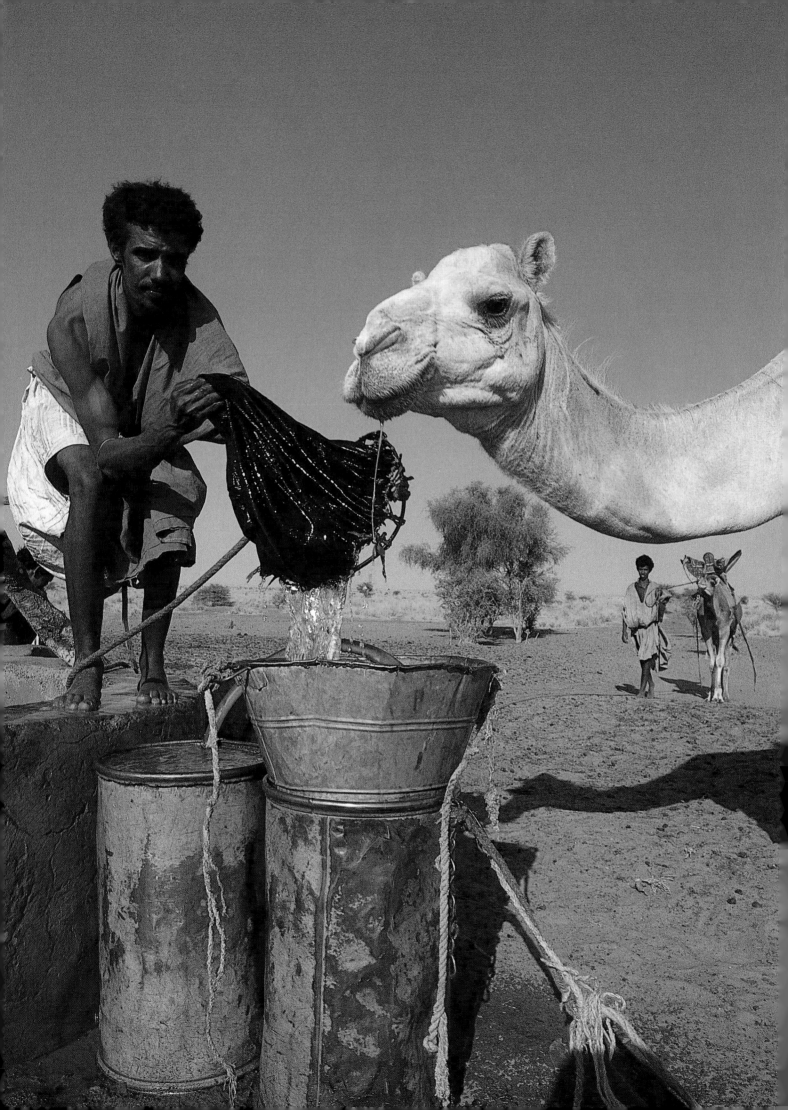

LEFT: Water sources in the Hammunat's territory are few and far between and may be several days' journey from the camp. Usually only men and boys accompany the herds to wells, although women can go but will never draw water. Sometimes water is drawn by hand; sometimes, especially when wells are very deep, a pulley system operates. The men are also responsible for fetching water for human consumption which is stored in large metal drums.

RIGHT: Goat-skin buckets, waterproofed with animal fat, are used to draw the water from the well. It is then poured into metal bowls from which the animals drink.

Hammunat's diet – which is limited; many women and children suffer from malnutrition – is made up primarily of milk and related products like yogurt, sour cream and butter. Although women never milk animals, they are responsible for storing and churning the milk. Meat, although rarely consumed outside religious festivals or marriages and baptisms, is provided by the Hammunat's herds or by hunting. Only men and circumcized boys can slaughter or hunt animals while women are responsible for the distribution of meat. The Hammunat supplement their diet with rice and with millet which they buy ready ground and which is cooked only by women. On the other hand, both sexes can make bread, which is made from flour and water and cooked directly on the fire, and prepare meat and tea.

Making and mending water and milk containers, or other objects such as drums, from animal hides is also an important women's activity. The cleaning, skinning and tanning techniques employed require considerable knowledge of the plants to be used. Certain women also have an extensive knowledge of traditional medicine or may be midwives.

It would be a mistake, however, to presume that women only spend their time in and around their tents since certain activities do take them beyond the confines of the camp. If the men are absent, the women may have to tend the herds of young sheep and goats, although this is rare. Or if they have time, women may travel to visit relatives and friends, or their holy men, or to attend weddings and baptisms in other camps and nearby towns. Women, moreover, play an important part in the social life of their families and the camp at large. Indeed, one of the most striking aspects of the role of women among the Hammunat and similar groups in Moorish society is their important and respected social position. Women interact with men beyond their family groups and can entertain men who are strangers in the camp both in the presence of their husbands and alone. It is common to see men and women drinking tea, discussing plans and the day's events or gathering around camp fires to listen to music. In this respect Moorish society is unlike some other Muslim and Arab cultures where men and women are segregated. Nonetheless, in spite of the fact that contact between men and women is relatively easy and relaxed,

RIGHT: Music is an important part of the Hammunat's social life, although usually only the women drum, sing and, more rarely, dance. The Hammunat's only musical instrument is the drum, which is made from cow skin stretched over a wooden base. The Hammunat's songs are sung poems (all Moors love poetry) on a variety of themes – love, politics, the history of the tribe, wars, places in the desert and religion.

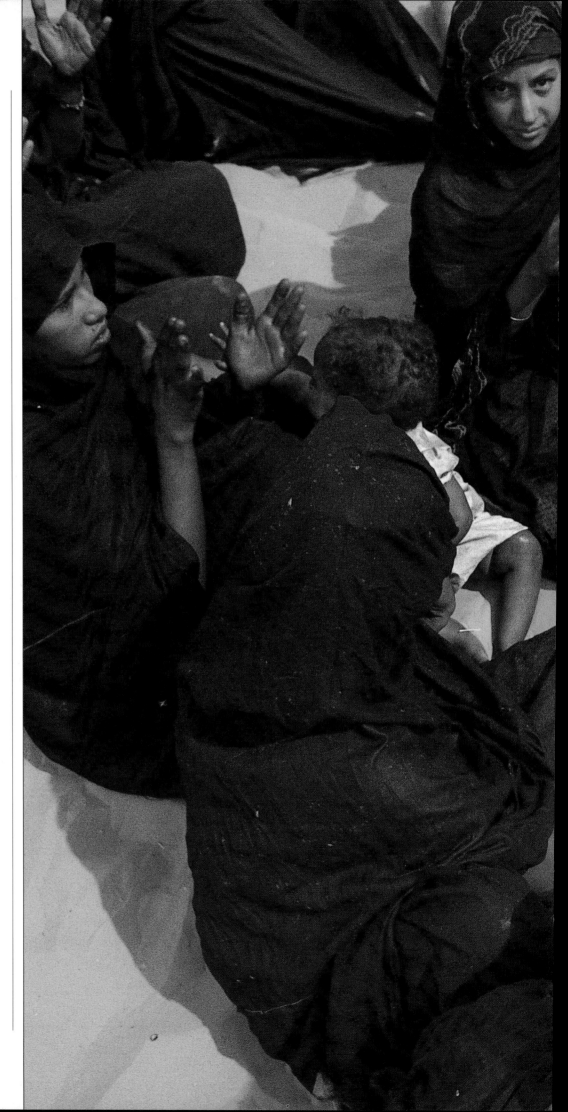

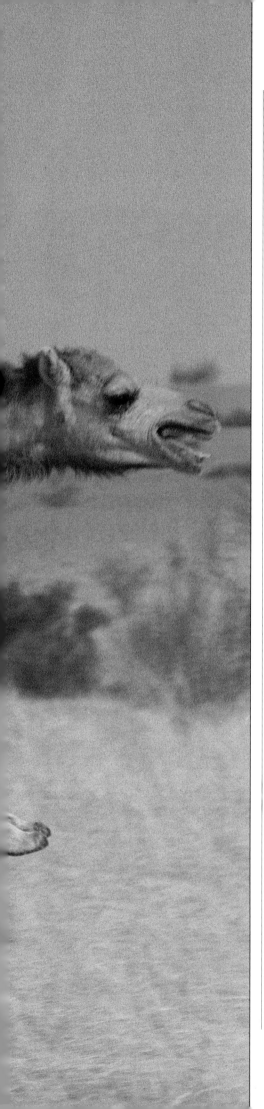

there are certain codes of behaviour. Relationships between people of different generations can be formal, and this is particularly so among men. Newly married couples will never speak to one another in the presence of people older than themselves and the relationship of the husband and wife to their respective in-laws is highly formal. A recently married man, for instance, never eats or drinks with his mother-in-law and completely avoids his father-in-law.

Both work and leisure activities nonetheless tend to separate men and women. Women seated in their tents, in the shade of a tree or on the back of a dune, spend their free hours playing a game unique to women known as *seeg* which is set up by tracing lines in the sand and played with counters of camel dung and broken pieces of grass. Or they may help each other to plait their hair and decorate each other's hands and feet with henna or drum and sing together. Men may play a game called *dhamit*. This, too, is traced in the sand and resembles draughts. Or they may sit together discussing their herds or lost camels and plans for moving.

Most of the time, though, men are absent from the camp for at least part of the day and sometimes for longer periods. This is because most work connected either with herd management or involving mobility is carried out by men and young boys. A typical day's activities for a Hammunat man will start before dawn after prayer by milking the herds. Then he puts on the females' belts and covers (that cover the teats of their animals to prevent their young suckling them) and sets the herds loose to graze. The camels set off to pasture unminded unless they are being taken to water at a well, although the herds of sheep and goats are always accompanied. Later, towards mid-morning, the man leaves to join his herd. He stays with his animals until around sunset, when he directs the herd back to the camp collecting firewood along the way. The sheep and goats are milked soon after nightfall and the camels late at night.

On some occasions men may stay away for longer periods of time – for example, when they take the herds to be watered at distant wells, go hunting or looking for lost animals, or visit herds that are grazing in other parts of the area. At other moments men spend time away in towns buying provisions, working or trading. Nevertheless, the presence of some men is always required in the camp because only they can milk, slaughter and fetch water. As long as a family includes several males this is not too much of a problem because tasks can be divided. This is one of the main reasons why, although daughters are loved and valued, the Hammunat prefer to have sons, and a family that has several sons is considered very fortunate. This allows an elderly father to spend much of his time in the camp while his sons mind and water the herds. A family with few, very young or no sons, by contrast, is obliged to rely on help from relatives, other members of the camp or – if they have the means – hired hands. Although members of the camp share some common tasks such as fetching water, men's work done for others is usually remunerated by gifts or payment in kind. For example, a man who helps a woman while her husband is away or who minds someone else's herds will be paid in kind for his efforts or given gifts.

Economic relations among the Hammunat are centred around the ownership of herds. Animals, which constitute the main source of wealth, are owned by individuals rather than by the tribe as a whole, and are acquired mainly through inheritance, giftgiving and at the time of marriage. Although members of a family often herd their animals together and share the animal produce, only the owner has the right to sell or split the herd. An individual's wealth is calculated almost entirely by the size of his or her herds, and is known as the 'wealth of blood'. The Hammunat make a clear distinction between this and monetary wealth.

LEFT: Breaking-in a young camel. Although most of the herd is used for milking, some animals are broken in to be ridden or used as beasts of burden. Before a saddle can be put on the camel, the animal must be trained to accept a weight on its back.

Making Essentials

Like nomadic tribes the world over, the Hammunat are skilled at making many of the things they need from materials found around them. (Other items such as bowls, cooking utensils, saddles, clothes, tea and sugar are bought from artisans who live with the Hammunat, or in nearby villages or towns.)

RIGHT: The mats which are sometimes used to cover the ground area of the tent are made by the women from strips of palm. Strips of leather are included in the design – partly as reinforcement, partly as decoration.

LEFT: This man is making rope from camel's hair by twisting the fibres together.

BELOW: Water containers are made from goatskin. Different techniques are used to treat and clean skins. In one method a plant known as asabay (*Leptadenia pyrotechnica*) is rubbed on the skin and left overnight. The next day the fleece can easily be removed. It is then dried, tanned and sewn up.

RIGHT: The finished container is filled with water to ensure that it is watertight.

In recent years, however, the Hammunat have come to see the limits to their traditional concept of wealth. This is because although the Hammunat rely on their herds for many of their consumption needs, essential items, such as clothes, tents, utensils and some foods, have to be bought. In many cases the only way to obtain cash is by selling animals. This makes the Hammunat rather vulnerable to fluctuations in the market prices of animals. There is no doubt that the cash economy has become increasingly important among the Hammunat. Marriage payments, for instance, which tend to be high, have become partly monetarized; and services and goods from traditional artisans, which were formerly paid for in kind, are now paid for mainly in cash. Another area affected is herd management. In the past, if individuals lost their animals through poor herd management or disasters such as drought, their relatives would, through a system known as *mniha*, help them to avoid having to settle by lending them animals whose milk and products they were entitled to consume. Recent evidence suggests, however, that there is an increasing tendency among the Hammunat, as elsewhere in Mauritania, to employ impoverished relatives or tribesmen, or outside workers such as the Tuareg, as hired herders.

The Yearly Nomadic Cycle
'The move follows the milk' HAMMUNAT SAYING

When asked why they move, the Hammunat reply that moving is determined by the needs of their animals; if their animals are to survive and produce milk for their young and for human consumption, they must have pasture. The decision to move and where to go is therefore always linked to the availability of pasture and water, and is taken by the men of a camp on the basis of information they have heard or have gathered from reconnaissance trips. Although the Hammunat follow roughly the same seasonal calendar and routes from one year to the next, the precise timing of moves and the routes taken are modified according to the conditions found in a given year.

In a fairly good year, when rainfall has been sufficient, the Hammunat spend the cool dry period between October and December in the north of their territory in a vast region known as Awker. Awker lies in the Saharan climatic zone and is traversed by a series of cliffs, known as the dahr of Oulata and the dahr of Tichit, which run south-east to north-west and mark the edge of the basin of Taoudenni. To the west Awker is crossed by series of dead water courses and fossilized valleys covered in sand. It is not uncommon to find here, as elsewhere in the Hodh and Mauritania, prehistoric arrowheads, stones, pottery and glass Venetian beads. To the north of Awker are rolling dunes which taper off into a vast desert region that extends to the frontiers of Algeria and where water points are few.

Although wells in Awker are days away from the camp, making life very harsh, the Hammunat, who virtually subsist on milk during the winter, consider Awker beautiful and appreciate the excellent grazing that their animals find there. The salty plants, *shat* (*Stipagrostis pugens*) and *hadh* (*Cornulaca monacanta*) provide enough nutrients for camels to go without water for long periods and, apart from milk-giving females, camels are often left to graze untended in this period. It may seem curious that the Hammunat let their herds graze unminded and they themselves admit that one of the disadvantages of their herding techniques is that camels are frequently lost. But they also claim that it is a waste of time to guard herds too closely since they will eventually always find their way to wells. In any case the men find lost animals by following their tracks, which they can read with impressive skill, or through information from other nomads who have seen them or found them in their herds. Although some herd rustling does exist, all camels carry a brand mark

RIGHT: Tea was introduced into Mauritania in the nineteenth century and since then it has become an indispensable part of the Moors' social life. Tea-drinking sessions punctuate the day and always greet the arrival of guests. The tea is brewed with sugar in small enamel pots and is drunk from small glasses.

and the sheep and goats a particular sign that immediately identifies them as belonging to a particular family and faction of the tribe.

Most of the Hammunat usually spend up to two months in Awker, although some groups spend much of the year there, moving from the wells around Oulata to pastures as far away as Tiris when conditions permit. An important activity during this period is the collection of *emersal* – a mixture of salty, crystallized sand and earth formed from water evaporation in the low valleys around the wells of Wraykika and Taguraret. *Emersal* is fed to animals and the Hammunat either store it or send it in caravans to be fed to their herds further south or to be sold in Mauritania and Mali where it is sometimes exchanged for millet. At this time the Hammunat, who move fairly frequently, may also visit the ancient caravan towns of Tichit and Oulata on the edge of Awker to water their animals, buy provisions or visit the tomb of the Muslim saint, Shaikh Sid'Ahmed al Bekkay, in Oulata.

Towards the end of winter, while the weather is still fairly cool, and sand storms start to be frequent, the Hammunat start to move south through a region which they call the Baten, meaning 'stomach'. (The Moors consider the landscape resembles the contours of the human stomach.) The Baten consists of dunes and sandy plains. As well as dry grass, a considerable number of plants, bushes and trees are found in this region, such as varieties of acacia and teyshit (*Balanites aegyptica*) whose thorny branches and fruit provide good grazing and excellent wood. Before the droughts of the late 1970s this area, which now resembles scrub land, was more fertile and had many more trees and creeks. Nonetheless vegetation that no longer exists elsewhere in Mauritania has survived here, making it one of the last remaining viable grazing areas for large herds of camels, sheep, goats and even cattle. The wells in this area are more accessible than those in Awker, but water is always scarce.

In this period the Hammunat move about every ten days to two weeks, each time going between three and ten kilometres further south. A typical move takes place in the morning after breakfast and it usually takes about one to two hours to pack up. Women take down and fold up the tents and, with the help of their husbands and children, load the family's possessions on the back of camels. The tent, its long wooden poles, metal trunks, mats, cushions, blankets, water skins, and various utensils are either tied to or placed under or on the *rhal* and are all carried by one camel. The heavy metal water drums are placed on another, and it's rare that a family

LEFT: The camels are milked by the men at dawn and late in the evening around 10 p.m. Milk is the most important part of the Hammunat's diet. It is drunk fresh and is also used to make butter, sour cream and yogurt, and a kind of cheese. If the lack of pasture prevents the animals from giving milk then the people's very existence too is threatened.

will need more than two camels for the move. When the preparations are over, women climb on to the already standing camels, and their small children are handed up to them.

Men and young boys walk leading the camels or accompany the herds which follow at some distance. Often the final destination is chosen only on arrival in the area. Although to the uninitiated eye the landscape seems incredibly monotonous the Hammunat, who have a remarkable sense of direction, know it intimately, naming areas after nearby wells or geographical features such as a cluster of trees or unusual dune formation. In deciding where to camp they consider a number of factors: the distance from other camps (which, although often in sight, are never closer than half a kilometre), the availability of firewood, the presence of hyenas, wolves or jackals who may attack the herds of sheep and goats and, most important, the location of pasture for their animals. Most often camps are set up on the backs of dunes because of the abundance of thorny grass, known as *initi* (*Cenchrus biflorus*). Once the families arrive at the camp they choose where to pitch their tents and start to unload. Setting up the tents is done by the women and girls and takes about one hour. Once the tents are up, both men and women set about making the enclosures in which the herds of young sheep and goats are kept at night. By this time, it is usually mid-afternoon and people tired by the hard work relax and make tea.

The Hammunat continue to move through the Baten area until the end of their spring, or *tiviski* as they call it, which precedes the beginning of the hot summer period. Eventually these moves take them near to Nuwal, an old well whose salty waters are renowned throughout Mauritania and northern Mali for their healing properties and beneficial effect on camels. At this time of year camels that have been left to graze in Awker or have been lost tend to find their way to Nuwal.

In the early 1980s, at a time of devastating drought, members of the Hammunat built a village at Nuwal marking one of the earliest attempts to settle among the tribe. Disaster struck, however, when the well water became too salty for human consumption and several deaths followed. At this point, with the help of the Mauritanian authorities, the inhabitants of Nuwal moved a couple of kilometres south and founded two villages within about two kilometres of each other. One of these they renamed Nuwal, the other Tuwil. The now abandoned Nuwal, with its derelict houses and cemetery, presents a striking desolate image but has retained its importance as a well for herds of camels, cattle, sheep and goats which are often seen drinking there in their hundreds. The two new villages, which each have a population of no more than several hundred, could be described as the capital of the Hammunat and the nomads often go to the weekly market at Tuwil to buy provisions.

If pasture is sufficient the yearly nomadic cycle of Hammunat may take them no further south than Nuwal, and they will remain in its environs moving less frequently throughout the hot summer months. During this period men may go into the nearby town of Timbedra, or to Mali, to trade. When the rains, which usually fall between June and September, arrive the men rejoin their families, and relatives who live in town come and spend time in the desert. This time of year, when the landscape turns a startling green and the dust and sepia-like film that hangs over the desert is washed away, is the Hammunat's favourite. Their herds prosper and milk becomes abundant. Camps are pitched closer together and there is a holiday atmosphere with young people meeting at night to drum, sing and recite poetry. Although marriages take place all year round, the rainy season is the preferred time. Towards the end of this season, in about September, the nomads resume their trek back north, moving rapidly and almost daily over the several hundred kilometres to their winter pastures.

Territory and Neighbours

The area known as the *trab al Hammunat* – land of the Hammunat – is associated historically with the Hammunat, and is bordered by Timbedra in the south, the limits of Awker to the east and north, and Umm Layadh to the west. The Hammunat

OVERLEAF
Wedding preparations. The bridegroom (dressed in white) jokes with his friends. Hammunat weddings are elaborate affairs. Held at the bride's camp and lasting a day and a night, they are a focus for groups of family and friends from far afield.

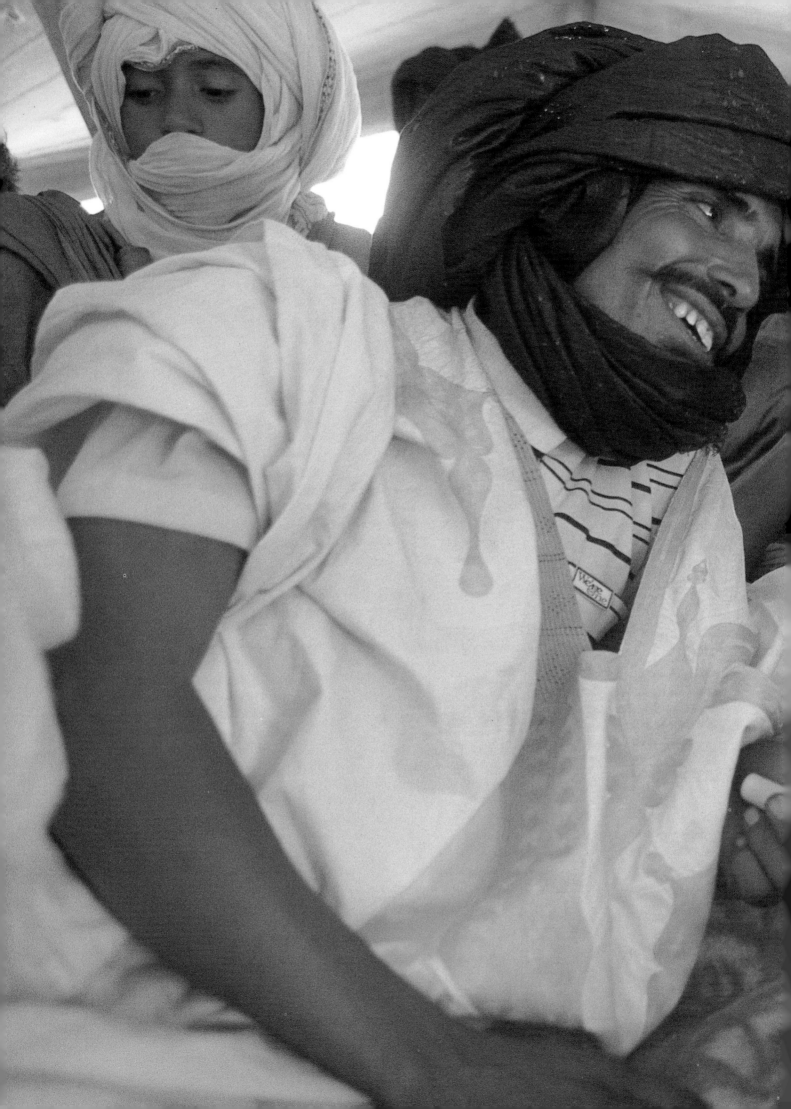

LEFT: Henna is used as a form of body decoration by Hammunat women, as it is in Arab societies throughout the Middle East and Muslim societies of West Asia. The leaves of the henna plant are dried and ground to a powder which is then pushed through a cloth to grind it finer.

RIGHT: The henna powder is mixed with water to form a paste which can then be painted on to the skin. It is used by Hammunat women for decorative purposes, particularly on festive occasions like weddings, or to greet husbands when they return from journeys. Henna is only applied to the hands and feet. The various designs have names such as the mouth of the camel, the tarmacced road, the basin and so on. Younger women and girls tend to trace more elaborate designs than the older women. Henna is also used as a traditional cure for circulatory and skin problems, and is believed to be very soothing.

are greatly attached to this area where most of their dead are buried, and where their wells and now villages are found. They consider that they collectively have privileged access to its pastures and wells. Land is not owned and the divisions of the tribe into factions do not correspond to territorial distinctions, so the Hammunat are free to move and camp where they like. Indeed, it is common to find camps belonging to distinct factions side by side in any part of the territory. However, although some wells are owned collectively by the Hammunat, others are associated with the individual factions and families that dug them and this can cause problems. Throughout the territory, the only water sources are wells, which are often very costly to dig and maintain because water is so far from the surface. Although in principle access to these wells is free and open to all, at times of drought when water is particularly scarce, or if wells are frequently used or crowded, the owners can claim privileged access or impose charges. Invariably such situations cause enormous tension and disputes, sometimes violent, erupt.

Moreover, groups from other Moorish tribes, such as the Kunta, Mechdouf, Laghlal, Awlad Nasser, Ijuman and Awlad Billa, live as nomads in the Hammunat's territory. Attracted mainly by the waters of Nuwal and the pastures of Awker, members of these tribes move freely throughout the territory – although here again disputes can emerge in times of hardship. Individuals from these tribes are often closely linked to the Hammunat through historical alliances and marriage and may live in Hammunat camps. This is particularly so in the case of the Kunta, who are the Hammunat's religious leaders and spiritual guides.

Just as the members of other tribes move through the Hammunat's territory, in years when pastures are insufficient the Hammunat move south in the summer into the territory of the Mechdouf. Because of the close historical relationship between the two groups the Hammunat tend to perceive this area, which runs from around the large town of Timbedra to the Malian border, as an extension of their own; and some of the Hammunat have settled in Timbedra and work there as animal traders. The region, which lies in the Sahelian climatic zone and where agriculture as well as cattle raising is common, is more densely populated than the Hammunat's own territory. This brings the Hammunat in contact with ethnic groups such as the Peul and Bambara, both in Mauritania and Mali.

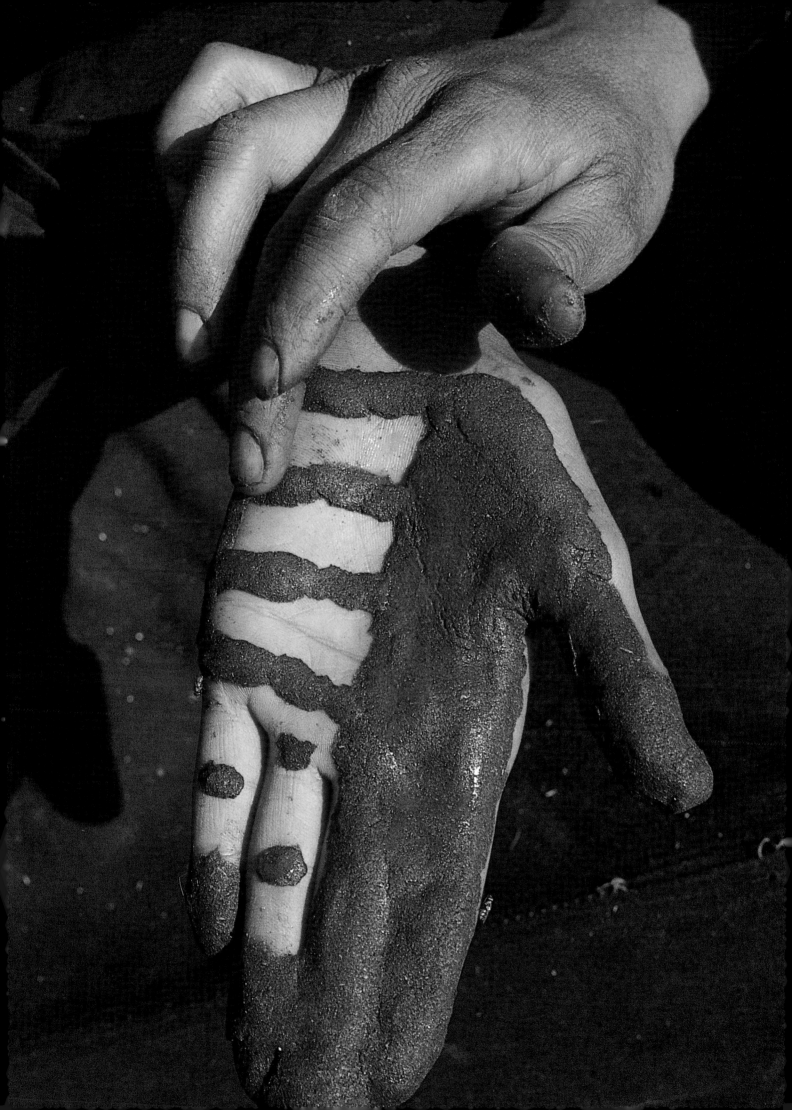

Recent Changes

In many parts of the world, nomads are ethnic minorities within their own country and face hostility from both settled peoples and even governments. Mauritania, however, is mainly populated and governed by Moors who share a common language, culture and nomadic background. Groups like the Hammunat, therefore, are not perceived as posing any threat and have in the past mainly been left to their own devices. Yet because of their continuing success as nomads, the Hammunat have been placed, ironically perhaps, at a disadvantage vis-à-vis many other Moorish tribes. Their lack of experience in anything other than livestock herding and trading, and the fact that few of their children have ever been to school, means that they are very poorly represented at the level of the national administration.

Both these factors seem to have played a part in the decision by certain of the Hammunat to construct a village in Nuwal in 1981. Members of the Hammunat who live there claim that it was both the drought, which ruined many families, and the desire to educate their children and gain a foothold in the administrative power structures of the country that prompted them to settle. Moreover, although the Hammunat had experienced droughts before, the drought of the early 1980s was an enormous shock to them. It gave them a sense of the potential fragility of their nomadic lifestyle and encouraged them to search for alternatives.

A decade later, the new villages of Nuwal and Tuwil now have schools, clean wells, basic health care facilities, shops and, in the case of Tuwil, a weekly market. Some of the Hammunat who have settled there have found new professions as traders, shop keepers and teachers; and attempts, to date mostly unsuccessful, have been made to introduce agriculture. The traditional chiefs of certain factions of the tribe, who were among the first to settle in old Nuwal, have found a new role as the elected mayors of Nuwal and Tuwil, as part of the government's attempt to install democracy on a local level. This last development has given the Hammunat a more institutional framework for settling their disputes and voicing their grievances.

Nevertheless, it has not been easy for the former nomads to settle, and settlement in Nuwal, Tuwil and other villages like Umm Layadh has remained fairly limited. The majority of the Hammunat, whose resourcefulness and hardiness cannot be underestimated, have remained nomadic, and were able to survive the drought by moving to Mali or by briefly settling before resuming their nomadic life. It has also been argued that the fact that there are now fewer nomads in the aftermath of the drought has reduced the pressure on pastures making life for those that remain more viable. However, it is clear that the nomadic Hammunat themselves pose a number of questions around the long-term viability of their lifestyle. One of their main dilemmas is the question of children's education: if, on the one hand, they send their children to school there is a danger that both an important source of labour power and the skills required to maintain the nomadic lifestyle will be lost. If, on the other hand, the drought, which is perceived as a calamity sent by god, returns they will be ill equipped to deal with the consequences if they remain uneducated. In spite of these fears and the undeniable harshness of their lives, the Hammunat continue to place a high value on their nomadic lifestyle and show few signs of giving it up. In the long term this may be helped by the policies of the Mauritanian government which, alarmed at the rate of sedentarization and urbanization throughout the country, has begun to pay more attention to problems that groups like the Hammunat face. A project for pastoralist associations, funded by the world bank, marks a new approach in the way that international organizations are thinking about nomadic pastoralists. The project, which covers the whole of Mauritania and is soon to be repeated in Mali, aims to provide veterinary services and animal feed to pastoralists, to improve and revitalize the pastoral economy, and to protect the environment. Although it remains to be seen what effects the plans for pastoralist associations will have on groups like the Hammunat, it is to be hoped that they will help them to continue their nomadic life for as long as they desire.

RIGHT: An old Hammunat woman. The old are greatly respected in Hammunat society and are looked after by their children and other relatives.

OVERLEAF
Around sunset the camel herd is driven back to the camp from its daytime pasture.

THE
TURKANA
OF KENYA

DR J TERRENCE McCABE

The cattle-herding Turkana live in the semi-arid desert of the Rift Valley of northern Kenya. After the great droughts of the 1980s, their herds are once more up to strength — but it is only their extraordinary understanding of their animals and their environment that has enabled them to survive.

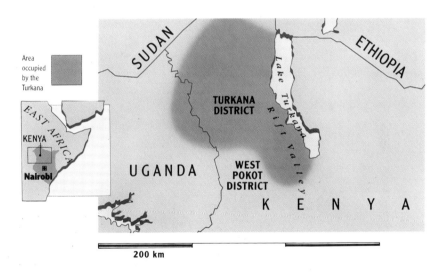

Area occupied by the Turkana

EAST AFRICA

KENYA

Nairobi

SUDAN

ETHIOPIA

Lake Turkana

Rift Valley

TURKANA DISTRICT

UGANDA

WEST POKOT DISTRICT

KENYA

200 km

LEFT: Camel's milk, in the dry season sometimes mixed with blood, is the staple ingredient in the Turkana's diet, providing most of their nutritional needs.

EVER SINCE EUROPEANS first visited Turkanaland in the late 1800s, they have been fascinated by the Turkana. First popularized as aggressive, treacherous and warlike in von-Hohnel's account of Count Teleki's expedition to what is now northern Kenya and southern Ethiopia, they have retained a reputation for being unco-operative and quick to fight. Their reputation was enhanced by their strong resistance to British rule and by frequent reports of raids and counter-raids between the Turkana and their pastoral neighbours. Although reports of aggressive, 'savage' Turkana can still occasionally be found, they misrepresent a people who are, in fact, friendly, open, intelligent and quick to laugh. I have been working with a number of Turkana families for more than ten years and am still amazed at the extent to which these supposedly difficult people have let me into their lives.

There is no doubt that their lives are hard. Pictures of hungry Turkana children were commonly portrayed in fund-raising efforts by charitable organizations in the early 1980s, leading to another misrepresentation of the Turkana as a destitute population of failed pastoralists. In reality, most of the pastoral Turkana survived the recent droughts as they have survived previous ones – by moving frequently and by depending upon each other. Food was scarce, livestock were dying, people were hungry, but they managed and their herds have recovered. What is interesting about the Turkana is not their past glory and modern failure, but their success. In this chapter I try to present a picture of the Turkana as I know them: not as the warlike nomads of the past, nor as the destitute pastoralists of the modern age, but as traditional pastoralists coping with a harsh environment and a rapidly changing world.

The Turkana and their Neighbours

The Turkana are one of a group of related peoples who speak a mutually intelligible language. This group, known to anthropologists as the Karimojong cluster or the Ateker group, also includes the Karimojong, Jie and Dodoth in Uganda, the Nyangatom in Sudan and Ethiopia, and the Toposa and Jiye in southern Sudan. Linguistic evidence suggests that all these tribes originated in northeastern Uganda and gradually dispersed into their present locations between the sixteenth and nineteenth centuries. Although they have much in common due to their common origins and their dependence on livestock, inter-tribal relations are characterized by shifting alliances and frequent hostilities.

ABOVE: The Turkana move regularly throughout the year in search of new pasture. When on the move, the men are responsible for the welfare of the herds and leave the camp at dawn with the animals, leaving the packing-up of the camp to the women.

RIGHT: The women and young children follow their menfolk shortly after dawn while it is still cool, their few material possessions loaded on to donkeys.

Setting up the *Awi*

On arrival in a new location, it is the women's job to set up camp. The Turkana build two types of shelter – the *ekol*, or day-time hut, which is no more than a brush-wood structure to provide shelter from the sun; and the *aki*, or night-time sleeping hut, which is only built when rain threatens. Slightly smaller than the *ekol*, the *aki* is covered with animal skins to make it warm and dry. Each married women builds shelter for herself and her children from brushwood saplings. The various shelters in the camp, including any corrals for the animals, are known collectively as the *awi*.

RIGHT: The first stage is to scrape out a series of holes in the earth, marking out the circumference of the hut.

RIGHT: Then saplings are cut down. These will be used to form the framework of the hut.

ABOVE: The saplings are placed in the holes and earth pressed down to hold them firmly in place. They are bent over and joined at the top to form a half-dome shape, and more saplings are woven in and out of this basic lattice framework. If the structure is to be an *ekol* (day-time hut), more saplings with green leaves are placed on top to provide shade.

LEFT: The *aki* (night-time hut) is built in the same way but is covered with animal skins to make it watertight.

The Turkana themselves recount their emergence as a distinct ethnic group in a myth which involves the wanderings of a Jie woman, Nayece, collecting wild fruits. Nayece settled on a hill near the Tarach river and remained there for some time. A bull lost in Jie country eventually found its way to Nayece's compound. Eight young men, Nayece's sons, followed the bull and found that the area offered both good grazing and an abundance of wild fruits. They settled there and eventually became the Turkana people.

Although the origins of the Turkana may be steeped in myth, it is clear that from the latter half of the eighteenth century to the middle of the nineteenth century, the Turkana gained strength and enlarged their territory at the expense of all their neighbours. They expanded their territory in the north and west and pushed the Samburu out of southern Turkana district into the area they now occupy to the southeast of Lake Turkana. During this period their reputation as fearless warriors spread throughout East Africa. Their fierceness and bravery in battle cannot be doubted, but two other factors greatly aided their ability to appropriate new territories. The first was that the Turkana livestock, living in the arid lowlands, were not

LEFT: Children are greatly valued in the close-knit Turkana community and are born into an extended family. Children are expected to play their part in herd management from a very early age, but this does not mean that they are regarded merely as a potential labour force. The love of this father for his children is evident.

devastated by the rinderpest epizootics which decimated the herds of most of the other pastoral peoples in the late 1800s. The second was that the Turkana gained access to rifles before their neighbours to the south and west, by way of the Abyssinians (Ethiopians) and the Italians.

The Turkana continued their expansion until they came into conflict with the British in the early twentieth century. The British aim during the colonial period was to prevent the Turkana from pushing south and disrupting British efforts to 'civilize' the agricultural people in the highlands area. In colonial documents the Turkana are often referred to as 'savage nomads' who must be kept in check. The British attempted to do this by sending occasional military expeditions into the northern regions to demonstrate their superiority and confiscate livestock in retribution for raids against the southern tribes. The most famous of these expeditions was the Labur patrol of 1918, in which more than 400 Turkana were killed and 20,000 cattle and 100,000 small stock confiscated.

Although the British did establish a few permanent outposts in Turkana country, their punitive expeditions were rarely followed by any effective government control. This gave the Turkana the impression that the role of the government was to punish and raid: the government was viewed as another enemy whose purpose was to steal livestock and kill people. Even today, this basic distrust has yet to be completely overcome in the more remote regions of Turkanaland.

Following independence, relations between the government and the Turkana gradually improved, but efforts at real 'development' did not occur until the 1970s. Unfortunately, severe droughts in 1979-81 and again in 1984-5 undermined development efforts, and outside aid switched from development to famine relief. Whether the relief efforts had a beneficial effect on Turkana society is debatable, but by 1989 the Turkana had recovered from the severe droughts of the previous decade and had resumed their hard, but successful, nomadic existence.

The Environment

Turkana district encompasses approximately 67,000 square kilometres of the floor of the Rift Valley in northwestern Kenya. It is bounded by Lake Turkana in the east, Sudan in the north, the Rift Valley escarpment which forms the Ugandan border to

RIGHT: Water is a precious commodity in the drought-ridden environment of the Turkana. In the *awi*, it is used only for cooking, drinking and, occasionally, washing young babies. (Adults do not wash themselves in the camp; the men bathe while watering the herds and the women when at the wells or a river collecting the daily water supply.)

the west, and West Pokot district to the south. The landscape has often been described as a moonscape, with vast expanses of volcanic rubble, sandy and gravel plains. It lies just north of the equator at about 350 to 450 metres above sea level. Among the plains are volcanic outcrops and mountains, sometimes rising 1,500 to 2,000 metres above the surrounding countryside. The vegetation varies according to altitude, with perennial grasses and trees dominating in the higher elevations and annual grasses and shrubs in the lower areas.

Ecologists believe that in the distant past this area was wetter than it is now and that the vegetation was similar to that of the Serengeti: grassy plains and acacia woodlands – a far cry from the harsh, desert-like landscape of today. Because the vegetation varies with altitude, the combination of mountains and plains results in a number of micro-habitats which can be used by the different species of livestock. Cattle, for example, are pastured in the mountains for most of the year; camels, on the other hand, require woody and leafy vegetation and so remain on the plains.

Equally important to the Turkana system of livestock management is the seasonal variation that, during good years, transforms the desert into a pastoral paradise. The rains usually occur between April and July, but it is impossible to predict exactly when they will come, if they will come at all, how long they will last, or where the rain will fall. It is not uncommon for the rains to fail once every three to five years, and a serious drought can be expected about once every ten years. On the other hand, there are years known for their exceptional rains when grass grows abundantly and the animals give more milk than the people can drink. The last year like this was 1975, called *Kachurokimak* by the Ngisonyoka of southern Turkana, which can be roughly translated as the year that the old women danced (because the locks were broken on the clouds).

The Section

There are approximately 200,000 Turkana people, divided into nineteen named sections (*ekitela*). Each section occupies a specific territory and the people who belong to a particular section have rights to the grazing and water resources contained within the section's boundaries. In northern Turkana, people and livestock tend to move freely across sectional boundaries, whereas in southern Turkana crossing from the territory of one section to that of another can only be done with the permission of the elders of the section to be entered. I believe that the principal reason for the difference in the rules governing boundary maintenance lies in the topographical differences between northern and southern Turkana district. In the north there are vast plains stretching to the horizon, with only a few mountain massifs far apart. During

LEFT: In the dry season, open water sources become increasingly rare as rivers and pools dry up and the Turkana are forced to dig wells. As the dry season progresses, they have to dig deeper and deeper, sometimes through rock, in order to reach water. These wells can be as much as seven to ten people deep. Water is passed up from one person to the next until it reaches the surface.

RIGHT: The deep wells are almost always fenced in by thorn bushes to stop the animals from breaking through in search of water and falling to an inevitable death at the bottom of the well. Watering of the herds is strictly controlled, with only a few animals allowed on the lip of the well at one time.

OVERLEAF
Turkana herdsmen round up an *awi's* herd of donkeys in preparation for the move to the next grazing ground. Donkeys are the Turkana's principal means of transportation. They are generally left to forage for themselves.

the dry season, people and livestock are forced to travel long distances to obtain grazing and water, frequently migrating above the escarpment into Uganda. In the south, however, the plains and mountains are in close proximity to one another, allowing the pastoralists to change habitats without moving great distances. Each sectional territory in the south contains a wet-season grazing area, a dry-season grazing area and a drought reserve. Only in particularly bad years are people forced to seek grazing or water in areas outside their own territory.

Like most other East African pastoralists, the Turkana have separate rules governing rights to forage and rights to water. There is no individual ownership of land; every member of a particular section has the right to pasture his animals anywhere within the sectional boundaries. However, there are very specific rules dictating who has the rights to individual water sources. Water can be found in open rivers when flowing, open pools as the rivers dry up, shallow wells dug through sand, deeper wells dug through sand and clay, and deep wells dug through sand, clay and rock. All open water and shallow wells can be used by anybody, but the deep wells can only be used by members of the family of those who dug the well, and close relatives or friends who have been given permission by the well owners. Outsiders often view pastoral land management as chaotic or without regulation when, in fact, it is in some respects highly organized.

The Awi

Every Turkana family lives in a homestead referred to as an *awi*. The *awi* consists of a man (the herd owner), his wives, their children, and often some dependent women (often an unmarried or widowed sister, or the herd owner's mother). Each married

LEFT: A very close bond is established between the children of the tribe and the animals they look after. This rapport enables them to feed straight from the goats at dawn, before the herds are driven to pasture, and again at dusk. Once the children have drunk their fill, the surplus is milked off for the adults.

RIGHT: Children become involved in the day-to-day work of the tribe from a very early age, taking an active part in herd management from as young as four or five. Although they have no specific duties, even at this age they know their animals well enough to tell if a single goat is missing from a herd of several hundred. This early – and instinctive – involvement in animal husbandry is the basis for the Turkana's lifelong attachment to their animals and an essential part of their education process.

woman builds two structures for herself and her children: an *ekol* and an *aki*. The *ekol* is a day-time sitting hut and consists of saplings arranged in a latticework in the shape of a half-dome. Once the latticework is complete, branches with green leaves are placed on top of the saplings. This provides a very comfortably shaded space with enough ventilation to let the breeze blow through. The *aki* is a night-time sleeping hut and is only built when there is the chance of rain. It, too, is constructed of saplings arranged in a half-dome structure, but it is smaller than the *ekol*. Animal skins are lashed to the outside of the *aki*, making it watertight. Each *awi*, then, contains an *aki* and *ekol* for each married woman, and a number of corrals for livestock; and sometimes, depending on the potential danger from predators, it is surrounded by a thorn fence.

The Turkana ideal is for a man to marry as many women as he can afford, and wealthy Turkana men frequently have five or more wives. Although this type of marriage pattern seems difficult for Western people to appreciate, the Turkana have as much difficulty understanding why a Western man should only be able to marry one wife. Co-wives help each other when one is sick or unable to work, they share food, and also share in the bridewealth when a daughter is married. The management of large herds of several species of animal requires a substantial labour pool, and I have been told many times that without many children a man has little or no chance of success. Marriages are, however, very expensive in Turkana society. When a man wants to marry he first discusses the arrangement with the prospective bride's father (and sometimes with his first wife). If the father finds the suitor acceptable, he will then discuss how many animals must be given to the bride's family in compensation

for the loss of their daughter. This practice, called bridewealth, helps to redistribute resources and also makes female children very valuable to the whole family. Unlike many other cultures in which daughters are either unwanted or discriminated against, Turkana girls are loved and valued. It is not uncommon for a bridewealth payment to consist of 20 to 50 camels, 20 to 50 cattle, and 100 to 200 goats and sheep. This is an exceptionally high bridewealth payment by East African standards (a typical bridewealth payment among the Maasai, for example, is seven cattle), and means that the groom has to ask for assistance in collecting animals from all his friends and relatives. All those who contribute to a bridewealth payment form the basis of a network of relatives and friends who give livestock to one another in times of need; and this is one of the most important social institutions in Turkana society.

Most Turkana men have separate herds of camels, cattle and small stock (goats and sheep are herded together). During the wet season all these animals are kept in the *awi*, in a separate enclosure for each herd. As the dry season sets in, the livestock are separated into species and taken to areas which best suit their particular forage and watering needs. Thus the family and their livestock coalesce and disperse according to the season, a fact which dominates much of Turkana social life.

Seasonality

All Turkana look forward to the wet season. It is a time of plenty, a time for feasting, a time for marriages, a time for dancing, a time for relaxing. The wet season begins slowly, with storm clouds building daily. Sometimes that is all they do, teasing the people with an anticipation which is unfulfilled. More often, however, rains cover Turkana district, frequently announcing their arrival with intense, violent thunderstorms. Rivers flow, recharging the wells that have gone dry during the previous months. The vegetation responds quickly, sending up fresh green shoots within days of the rains commencing.

Soon after the livestock begin eating the new nutrient-rich vegetation, their condition improves and their milk flow increases. This is also the time when the livestock give birth, and as the wet season progresses the *awi* is filled with the sounds of young animals crying for their mothers and the reassuring calls of the mothers returning from the day's grazing. Because vegetation is abundant, all the family's livestock herds return to their home area, which is usually located on the plains. The return of family members who may have been absent for eight to ten months contributes to a feeling of contentment and well-being.

Families set up their *awis* close to one another forming neighbourhood groupings called *adakars*. During moon-lit nights, the call to come and dance can be heard coming from one of the *awis*. Young men and women gather together to sing and dance throughout the night. People sing in praise of livestock, about their land, and about good years.

The wet season is also the time for marriages and initiations. Marriages are elaborate affairs, often lasting for days. Livestock are transferred from the groom's to the bride's family, usually accompanied by prolonged haggling concerning the condition of a particular animal, and the exact number to be given to each relative. Oxen, castrated camels, rams and billy goats are slaughtered and eaten, sometimes locally brewed beer is drunk and, of course, the people dance. The marriage ceremony is considered complete when all the bridewealth has been transferred and the 'bull of the wedding' has been speared. The new wife usually moves into the *ekol* of her mother-in-law until she becomes pregnant with her second child, at which time she builds her own *ekol* and *aki* and becomes a fully fledged wife and mother.

Initiations are no longer the elaborate celebrations reported in early accounts of Turkana life. Unlike most East African pastoralists (and many agricultural groups as well), the Turkana do not circumcise either young men or women. The initiation (*asapan*) involves the young man symbolically discarding the material items associated with his youth – cloak, sandals, bracelets, etc. – and putting on new attire, given by his initiation father, which marks him as a man.

RIGHT: Camel's milk is drunk fresh and is a natural supplement to mother's milk. Gourds of milk are hung in the *ekol* to keep cool. The gourds are shaken to separate the butter fat from the milk; this is used for cooking, body decoration and to coat beads to prevent them from splitting in the heat.

BELOW: The Turkana have only started to herd camels in relatively recent times. From the very beginning they found them difficult to handle and control, which may explain why they are not normally broken in and used for transportation. Camels are milked twice a day, at dawn and at dusk, by the women of the camp. The camel's milk flow is started by a calf being allowed to suckle for a while. (The lactation period for a milking camel is 13 to 18 months.)

OVERLEAF

A Turkana encampment at dawn before the animals have been led off to graze. In this *awi* there are only camels, sheep and goats; the cattle are kept in another area where there is more grass. Whereas the greenery of the acacia trees appears abundant, there is little grazing here as the rains have been poor. The Turkana's stay here will be limited to a few days.

ABOVE: As less milk is available in the dry season, the Turkana supplement their diet by taking nutrient-rich blood from their animals. The cut soon heals – a prime example of the Turkana taking just what they need from their animals and environment and no more.

RIGHT: The blood is heated to solidify it. It is then eaten raw or drunk mixed with milk.

Wet seasons are times to enjoy the pastoral life: food is abundant and the family is together. Unfortunately, after a few months the grasses set seed and begin to dry and the landscape turns from green to yellow to brown as the vegetation withers and dies. Once the grasses lose their nutrients, the cattle are taken from the *awi* into the mountains where some green grass might still be found. Each herd is managed by a young man who may be accompanied by younger brothers or cousins. Several young men will herd their cattle together for protection against lions, hyenas and enemies, and for sociability. Herd managers are usually aged between eighteen and thirty and are responsible for all decisions concerning the welfare of the herd. The cattle are sometimes hundreds of kilometres from the main *awi* and the young men cannot depend on their fathers for advice.

As the dry season progresses, the herd owner must decide whether to separate his remaining livestock into smaller herds, or keep them together. If there is enough labour and conditions warrant, he divides his camels and small stock into a milking and a non-milking herd for each species. As with the cattle, these herds are managed by a young man who is responsible for their welfare. The herd owner tries to keep abreast of the situation in the satellite herds and to make the decisions, but often the herds are located far from the major *awi* and communication between herd owner and herd manager is impossible.

Both the satellite herds and the main *awi* move more frequently in the dry season. For some people nomadic movements bring to mind images of whole tribes moving vast distances across a barren landscape. For the Turkana, the decision to move is made by the individual herd owner. Many men may sit together and discuss the state of the vegetation and water or the danger presented by wild animals or enemies, but the decision of when and where to move rests on the individual. Sometimes it is felt that it is too dangerous to move as individual family units and *adakars* move together. More often, the lack of forage in the dry season means that each family has to move independently, although it is rare for a herd owner to keep his family and livestock completely isolated from the rest of the pastoral community.

Often the moves cover short distances – 8 to 10 kilometres at a time. A Turkana family may engage in these types of move twelve to fifteen times during the year (all the while the cattle and the non-milking herds of camels and small stock are moving independently). These short frequent moves reveal one of the keys to Turkana survival: the ability to adjust quickly to small environmental changes. The Turkana are keenly aware of their environment and remember the location of a brief shower which may have occurred weeks ago. Sons or brothers of a herd owner are frequently sent on scouting missions to assess the state of the vegetation for a particular species of livestock. Reports may come in stating that a particular valley has good forage for camels, but is not suitable for goats and sheep. A herd owner must then decide whether to divide his livestock and move to that location, to remain in his present location or to seek out a new area. The health of his livestock and the survival of his family depend on these decisions.

Not only is there less forage in the dry season, but water sources begin to dry up. In certain sections of the sandy river beds, people dig wells. It is usually the work of the women to water the livestock and thus to dig the wells. In the dry season women typically accompany the livestock to the wells every other day and work there for two to four hours, scooping up sand, gravel and water from the bottom of the well in a carved container called an *atubwa*. The *atubwa* is passed from one woman to another until it reaches the surface; the water is then poured into a small trough for the livestock to drink and the sand and gravel thrown to one side. As the water table falls, the wells gradually become deeper and wider. At the height of the dry season, the wells can be seven to ten people deep.

Along with the heat and the increased work loads, the Turkana have to cope with a significant decrease in the food supply during the dry season. Because there are few nutrients left in the grasses, the cattle and sheep stop giving milk within a

ABOVE: The more traditional Turkana are firm believers in ritual. The goat slaughtered in this photograph had belonged to the late head of the family. As the Turkana believe that it is wrong to take something that belongs to someone else, even after that person's death, the contents of the goat's entrails are daubed over the chest of every man, women and child in the camp to appease the spirit of the old man.

couple of months after the dry season begins. Although the camels and goats can still give milk, the amount available to the Turkana is far below that available in the wet season. The people adjust to this change by bleeding the livestock and consuming the blood, slaughtering animals (usually castrated males and older females) and collecting and eating wild fruits. Although this type of diet, especially the consumption of blood, does not seem particularly appealing to Westerners, it is actually quite nutritious. If they are near a trading centre and grain is available, the Turkana may also decide to sell some of their animals and purchase grain.

In severe dry seasons, there is often not enough food to feed both the immediate family and dependent relatives who may be living with them. When this happens, dependants have the option of moving to the *awi* of a more wealthy relative or seeking food in one of the settlements. It is socially unacceptable for a man who can spare food not to share it with relatives or friends who are in need, and wealthy men have very large 'families'.

Thus as the dry season intensifies, some *awis* experience a major shift in the human population. The herd managers and herd boys leave the *awi* to accompany

LEFT: The Turkana often eat meat – especially sheep and goats, as they are most reluctant to slaughter their larger animals. During the dry season, when there is less milk available, it is usually the castrated animals that are slaughtered first.

RIGHT: Noted for their lack of fastidiousness, the Turkana eat every possible part of the animal. The choicest tit-bits, like the head of the goat, are roasted immediately on an open fire. The rest is kept until required.

the non-milking herds, and the dependants of the poorer families leave to live temporarily with wealthier relatives or abandon the pastoral system until the following wet season. Sometimes a poor relation will stay with the *awi* in which he or she is living, but ask for the loan of a few animals for milk or to eat or sell. It is this willingness to share that has allowed the Turkana to survive severe dry seasons and droughts without outside aid.

Although they form the cornerstone of long-term survival for the Turkana, these social networks are in some ways fragile. Following the drought of 1979-81, relief agencies provided massive quantities of food for the people living in northern Turkana. I watched as thousands of people migrated into the relief camps rather than rely on their traditional social institutions. The temptation of free food was, for many people, irresistible. It seems rather ironic that the Turkana were able to resist the incursions of the colonial powers for decades, yet a significant proportion of the population became dependent on donated food aid in just a few years.

For many, a return to the pastoral system would prove to be extremely difficult. Unlike those who had remained in the pastoral system and begged or borrowed livestock and food from friends and relatives, those who left for the relief camps found that they had great difficulty in acquiring livestock to rebuild their herds. Friends and relatives were less willing to give or lend livestock to the famine camp residents than to those who had remained in the pastoral system, as they felt that those in famine camps would be unable to return to pastoralism. They also found that the bridewealth paid for their daughters was far less than it would have been if they had remained in the pastoral system.

The indigenous system of redistribution was beginning to break down, aided by the very efforts intended to help the pastoral people. Fortunately, the drought broke and many of the relief agencies re-evaluated the impact of their food distribution programmes.

Problem Solving

One of the questions frequently asked about people like the Turkana, for whom the independence of the individual is paramount and for whom there are no chiefs, political officers, or police, is how do they solve social problems? In any location there is always a place — usually referred to as the 'tree of the men' — where the old men gather. There issues of common concern are discussed and grievances are aired. A particularly serious matter may be scheduled for discussion and, because each case is unique, the assessment of guilt and retribution may be argued back and forth for hours. It is the old men who make the decisions and their word must be obeyed.

Not all grievances are scheduled for public debate, but the process is always the same. I witnessed an example of the Turkana method of problem solving recently, just before I returned from the field. I was staying with the family of a friend named Angerot. Angerot is in his forties and has built his livestock holdings from a very small inheritance into substantial herds of cattle, camels, and especially small stock. He is recognized as an expert livestock manager and a man of courage and intelligence. In other words, his opinion is respected. One morning, a commotion at a nearby *awi* caught our attention. The herd owner, Epa, had discovered that a goat had been stolen and he had found evidence of its slaughter and roasting. He was convinced that the people responsible were the herd boys of a family living just up the dry wash. It also turned out that the suspects were not from the Ngisonyoka section, but from the Ngibocheros who had left their areas because of drought. Angerot, Epa, and five other men confronted the boys and, after prolonged discussion, one of the boys admitted to killing and eating the goat. Epa at first demanded that nine big castrated goats be paid in retribution for the theft, but Angerot and the other men thought that this was excessive. They decided that a fine of five castrated goats would be a fair settlement, and this was paid. No outside forces were called in, no feelings of resentment and mistreatment remained on either side. The goal was to restore social harmony and ensure that the wronged party was treated fairly.

OPPOSITE: Elaborate hair styles were once an important feature of Turkana life. Now, as so few of the Turkana sport this traditional coiffure, professional 'stylists', usually members of the older generation, have to be employed from outside the *awi*. Styling often takes three hours or more. Clay is combed into the hair, and this holds it in place for up to three months. Patterns are combed into the hardening clay and, as a finishing touch, red ochre is painted on the front of the hair. The ostrich feathers worn by this man are an indication of his important status within the tribe.

Body Decoration

Body decoration is an important feature of all East African pastoralists – an art form that differs from one nomadic tribe to another. Hairstyles, beadwork, jewellery, body painting, scarification: all reveal the individual's tribal, marital and social status.

RIGHT: This old lady's ostrich eggshell beads and aluminium leaf earrings reflect her status as the oldest surviving wife of an *emeron* (witchdoctor) chief.

BELOW LEFT AND RIGHT: All Turkana undergo scarification from a very early age. In some cases it is done for medical reasons – as a traditional remedy for arthritis, rheumatism and other aches and pains. More commonly, as here, it is for decoration.

OPPOSITE: Body painting is commonplace among all East African pastoralists, especially among the women. Red ochre, mixed with liquid fat, is highly fashionable, and is applied to the hair and to the beads worn around the neck.

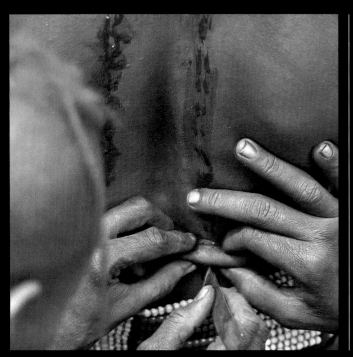

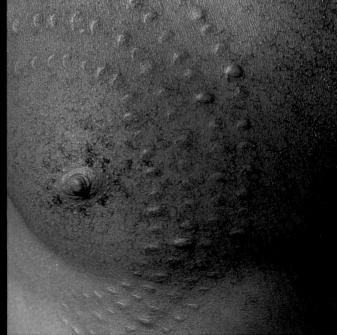

Environmental Impact

One of the major criticisms levelled at pastoralists is that they manage their livestock in an irresponsible manner which results in overgrazing and environmental degradation. I have been a member of a multi-disciplinary team of scientists who have been studying the impact of pastoral exploitation on the ecosystem in southern Turkana for more than ten years, and the only evidence of environmental degradation that we have found is in those areas immediately surrounding water holes and settlements. It is certainly true that environmental degradation has been observed in many other areas inhabited by pastoralists. In fact, one of the more degraded pastoral areas is the region inhabited by the Rendille, who live on the eastern side of Lake Turkana in an environment similar to that of the Turkana. However, the major difference between the Turkana and the Rendille is that the Rendille have, for the most part, been settled, while the Turkana remain nomadic. If one examines the areas where environmental degradation has been observed in conjunction with pastoralism, one frequently finds that the pastoral system has been greatly altered — either by settling the pastoral people, by restricting their traditional nomadic patterns, or by introducing new technologies (such as boreholes) without understanding the long-term consequences that can result from changing the balance between the land and the number of animals which can be supported on it.

Pastoralists have frequently been accused of managing their livestock without any rules because the land is common property rather than individually owned. This is known in the scientific and management literature as the 'Tragedy of the Commons' argument and has been the basis of many failed livestock development projects in Africa. The basic assumption in this argument is that in order for land to be developed it must first be privatized. It should be clear from the preceding discussion that the Turkana practise a complex system of livestock and land management. Pastoralists have been living in East Africa for five thousand years and have not destroyed the environments in which they have lived. Today they are subject to land encroachment from cultivators and conservation groups. Development planners attempt to restructure their system of land tenure and social organization. Governments try to sedentarize the people and restrict the movement of their livestock. Conservation groups assume that pastoralists must be removed from all areas that need to be 'protected'. And the pastoralists themselves are blamed for failed projects

ABOVE: This man's hairstyle has just been completed: the grey clay takes on a lighter tint as it dries out. Two holders for ostrich plumes, made from dried cow gut, are placed on top of his head.

RIGHT: A young girl is having her hair plaited and de-loused. Women rub ash into the hair to disentangle the locks that have become matted in fat. Up to the age of puberty, Turkana girls wear their hair 'Mohican style', with most of the head shaved clean.

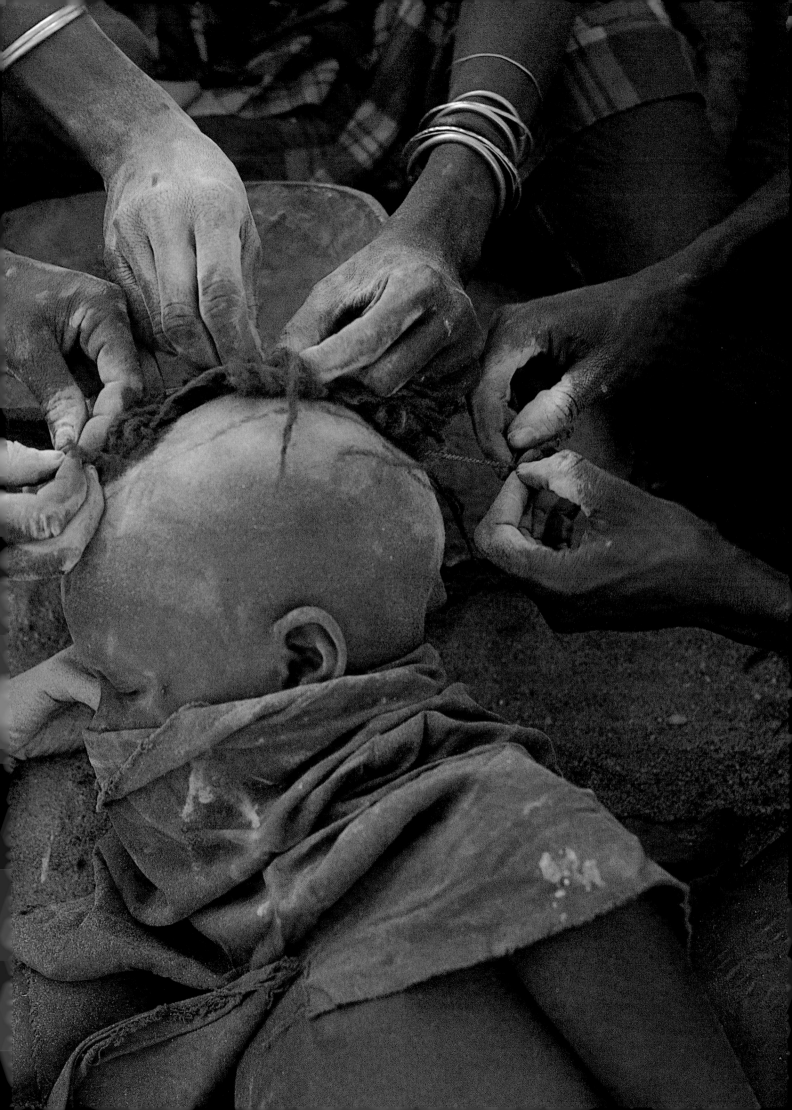

and environmental degradation. It is time to set the record straight on this issue and hopefully this brief discussion of Turkana life will be a small contribution.

Conclusion

In this chapter, I have tried to get away from the overly romantic notions which have often characterized accounts of nomadic peoples in the past. I have also tried to present the realities of life in a harsh environment frequently subject to drought. Life for many nomadic pastoralists is rapidly changing, and often not for the better. One of the reasons for their sedentarization and loss of traditional grazing lands is that development planners and government policy-makers view pastoral systems as incompatible with the goals of the modern nation-state. They view pastoral systems as environmentally destructive and economic failures with no place in today's development plans. I hope that those reading this chapter are given a different impression.

There is hope, however. The new five-year development plan for the Turkana does not advocate the complete sedentarization of the Turkana and recognizes the need for mobility in the management of livestock in this arid region. There is mounting scientific evidence that traditional pastoral systems may be as productive as many Western ranching operations. But there is still resistance, among both government officials and international donor agencies, to implementing livestock development plans based on traditional systems of land tenure and management. Hopefully the view of the Turkana presented here will help to offset misconceptions.

OPPOSITE: A young girl, her hair partially shaven and plaited, leans against a stick. (As nomadic herders, all Turkana carry sticks like this.) As she gets older, the number of strands of beads around her neck will increase year by year as an important part of her body decoration.

RIGHT: Standing on one leg was at one time distinctive pose of most East African pastoralists – a habit that is rapidly disappearing. Turkana women now seem to stand like this only while milking camels. The wood block carried by the man on the right is still commonplace among the Turkana and is used as a stool or head-rest.

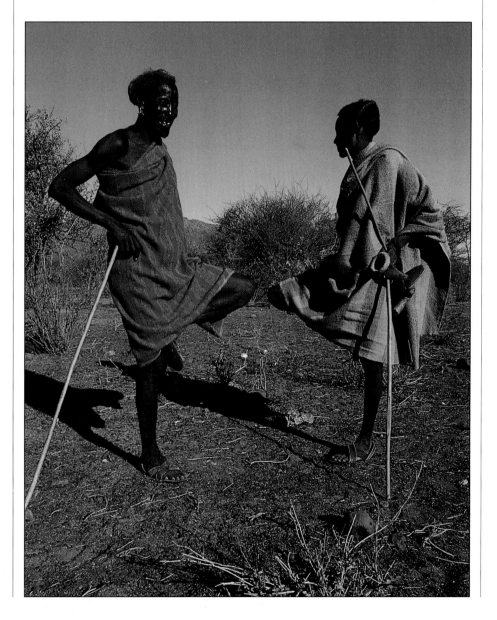

THE
HORSEMEN
OF MONGOLIA

STEVEN SEIDENBERG

The nomadic horsemen of Inner Mongolia are the last remnants of the Golden Horde of Genghis Khan who once ruled the largest land empire in the history of the world. Despite attempts by the Chinese authorities to integrate them into the rest of Chinese society, they cling to their centuries-old culture and traditions.

200 km

LEFT: The Mongols were renowned for their horsemanship a thousand years before Genghis Khan's nomadic army swept across the plains of Central Asia in the thirteenth century.

THE MONGOLS are one people living in several countries. They share a common language, history and culture dating back more than one thousand years. The high point of the Mongols' history was between the thirteenth and fifteenth centuries when they thundered out of the North Asian steppe and conquered the largest land empire in the history of the world. At its peak, this empire stretched from Vienna to Vladivostok and from Siberia to Burma. However, once the Mongols settled down to rule their conquests – as the Yuan Dynasty in China, the Mughal Empire of India, the Il-khans of Persia and the many Khanates of Central Asia – they quickly faded from history. The remnants of the original Mongol hordes are now spread throughout Central and North Asia, with the main concentrations living in the Mongolian People's Republic (formerly 'Outer Mongolia') and the Nei Monggol Autonomous Region of China ('Inner Mongolia'). Smaller numbers live in the other Autonomous Regions of China and in the Tuva ASSR in the Soviet Union.

The two Mongolias represent a formidable area. Inner Mongolia has an area of approximately 1.2 million square kilometres while the Mongolian People's Republic is about 1.6 million square kilometres. The Mongol population is, however, tiny. Estimates vary, but it seems the total number of ethnic Mongols does not exceed seven million. There are perhaps four million Mongols in China (3.4 million in Inner Mongolia) and a further two million in the People's Republic. There are less than a million Mongols in the Soviet Union. Thus the total population of Mongols in an area the size of western Europe is less than the population of London or Beijing.

It is difficult to generalize about the climate or environment of the continental-sized landmass of the Mongolias. One word, however, sums it up: severe. The climate is characterized by hot dry summers, very cold winters, low rainfall and high winds. Annual precipitation throughout much of the region is below 25 centimetres and in the southern portion (in which the Gobi is but one of the better-known deserts) it is almost negligible. The annual frost-free period is only about one hundred days in the People's Republic and only slightly longer in Inner Mongolia. Land that isn't desert is generally high plateaux. The mean elevation of the People's Republic is over 1500 metres; that of the Nei Monggol Plateau is only slightly less. Limited agriculture is possible in irrigated areas. The plateaux do, however, support extensive grasslands which provide ideal pastures for nomadic herders.

This chapter looks at Mongols in the vicinity of Xilinhot, the headquarters town of the Xilin Gol League. Xilinhot is roughly 450 kilometres north of the Great Wall and roughly the same distance north-east of Hohhot, the capital of Inner Mongolia. The Xilin Gol League covers an area of over 170,000 square kilometres (roughly one-third of the entire area of Inner Mongolia) and is subdivided into twelve districts. It has a population of approximately 800,000 (about a quarter of whom are Mongols).

The Family

In the normal course of events, each Mongol campsite is home to a single family unit (*ail*). Mongol families work independently of one another and come together only occasionally, during times of plenty.

There is a sexual division of labour within the *ail*. Men are responsible for the herding of large animals, for hunting, and for military and administrative activities. They make and repair the saddles, tackle, carts and weapons, make boots and milk mares. Women, however, do the lion's share of the labour. They are responsible for all domestic activities – for cooking, milking and making milk products (women have the dubious distinction of being 'the caretakers of the milk'). In addition, women husk millet, make domestic objects (such as cushions, rugs and drapes), collect dung and fashion it into fuelcakes, herd sheep and goats, and take care of young animals. And, of course, women are responsible for the care of children and old people. Activities involving both sexes include tanning hides, making felt, and, most importantly, making and breaking camp.

BELOW: Even today, the horse is central to Mongol culture and horse nomads are the cream of Mongol society. The two things the Mongols look for on their migrations are grass and water for their herds – both in abundance here.

Although Mongol families are constantly on the move, this does not mean that their children's lives are simply one long adventure. Children's chores begin at an early age. They learn to ride almost as soon as they can walk and, while still young, assume responsibility for the herding of the sheep and goats. They also help in the collection of animal dung that will be dried for use as fuel to cook their food and warm their tent or *ger*. Traditionally children lived with their parents until they were adults. With the increasing emphasis on the value of formal education, however, there are growing pressures for school-age children to leave their families and board in town so that they can attend school.

The Herds

The Mongols herd five different animals, known collectively as the *mal*: horses, cattle (which includes yak), camels, sheep and goats. Although the sheep is by far the most important animal economically, it is the horse that is central to the Mongols' very existence. Indeed, the horse pervades every aspect of Mongol culture.

Horse nomads are the cream of Mongol society. But not all Mongol families can afford to keep horses and those families without them are at both a social and functional disadvantage, with their ability to travel, hunt and herd severely

The *Ger*

The basic dwelling of the Mongols is known as the *ger*. (Europeans use the term 'yurt', but not the Mongols themselves.) The design of the *ger* has remained unchanged for centuries. It comprises a collapsible lattice of birch willows, which forms the walls, and a conical roof. The framework is covered with layers of felt for warmth. The flimsy-looking skeleton of the *ger* belies its strength. The *ger* is able to stand against the ferocious storms and winds of the steppes and is remarkably snug and dry even in the wettest of weather.

ABOVE: Some Mongols have shrines in their homes, often now with a picture or statue of Genghis Khan. Statues of the five animals of life, the horse, cattle, camel, sheep and goat, stand in front of the picture.

ABOVE: All cooking is done in a smaller *ger* which is also used as a store room. A hole (*öröke*) in the centre of the roof, which can be covered with a flap in bad weather, lets in light and also allows smoke to escape.

LEFT: An old man and his grandson inside their *ger*. The largest *ger* in the family's campsite is used both as a living area during the day and for sleeping at night.

RIGHT: The whole family – three generations – gathers together to listen to traditional songs. The man on the left is playing the *erhu*, or horse-head fiddle – a reminder of the importance still attached to the horse in Mongol society. Poems and songs are still written about the horse.

curtailed. And we must not forget that it was the horse that gave the Mongols the devastating mobility which enabled them to conquer such vast areas of land. It should be recognized, however, that their ability to flee from militarily superior foes may well account for the fact that the Mongols were never beaten in battle of overcome by conquest.

Mongol horses are small, but they are exceptionally strong and vigorous. They come in all colours and patterns – brown, black, white, grey, red, piebald, skewbald, dappled – although some are more highly regarded than others. The horse is kept as a mount and for milk. It is not eaten (although there is some evidence that the horse was sacrificed in religious ceremonies in the Mongols' pre-Buddhist days) and it is not used as a draught animal.

The centrality of the horse to Mongol culture is easily seen by the many specialized horse-related terms they have in their vocabulary. The Mongols have specific words for the colour, age, size, generation, etc. of their horses. For example, Mongols will speak of a *saaral* (white horse), *ke'er* (bay horse), *je'ered* (reddish-brown horse), *köke* (blue horse) etc. Each of these terms is used only to refer to a specific kind of horse. You could not use the word *je'ered*, for example, to describe the colour of the soil or of a brown-coloured cloth. This is in sharp distinction to the other great East Asian cultures: the Chinese and the Japanese have only one word for 'horse'.

In terms of numbers, camels are the least important of the Mongols' livestock. The camel is primarily used as a beast of burden either carrying household goods (and, indeed, the house itself), supplies, and those too young or too old to ride horses, or else pulling carts loaded with the same items. The camel is not eaten, and while its wool is used, it is only milked in extreme circumstances. Nevertheless, even far from the desert areas, most Mongol families tried to keep at least one camel. Mongolian camels are the Bactrian (two-humped) variety.

Various kinds of cattle (oxen, yaks) are kept by the Mongols. Like the camel, cattle are used as beasts of burden either carrying loads or pulling carts. However, cattle products (milk, hides, leather, meat and dung) play a far more important role than the camel's in the Mongol domestic economy. The yak is arguably the finest of the various cattle types available to the Mongols. Its milk is the richest in fats, its hide the most useful, and it is generally more active – especially at high altitude – than other breeds. As the Mongols become increasingly sedentary, however, new 'improved' (i.e. western) breeds of cattle are being introduced into Inner Mongolia. Whether they prove viable in the long term has yet to be established.

Sheep are the main herd animal. In addition to meat, sheep provide wool and leather. Sheep are the Mongols' main source of income and are sold not only for their meat but for their wool. The indigenous variety of sheep – the local 'fat-tail' sheep – is well adapted to the rigours of the Mongolian climate. (And the fat of the tail was traditionally an important part of the Mongol diet.) These sheep are increasingly being replaced, however, with 'improved' varieties that have come by way of Australia and the West. These grow larger than the indigenous variety (hence turning a greater profit in the marketplace) and produce both more and better wool. This is reflected in the official pricing structure, with wool from an improved sheep commanding a rate of 2.5 *yuan* per *jin* (a measure roughly equal to half a kilogram) from the State, while wool from indigenous sheep brings only 1.5 *yuan* per *jin*.

Goats have been herded by the Mongols for centuries, although Mongols prefer not to eat goat meat and their wool is no more profitable than that of sheep. Increasingly, however, Kashmiri goats – whose very fine wool *is* of great value – are herded in Inner Mongolia. This has made China one of the world's largest producers of cashmere wool. In view of their low economic value one suspects that the Mongols keep goats because they are the hardiest of the herd animals and are consequently best able to survive the extremes of the Mongol climate. As such they serve as a walking 'insurance policy' against the worst natural disasters.

It is extremely difficult to specify the size of the 'average' Mongol herd

RIGHT: It is common for three generations of a Mongol family to live and herd together. Grandparents migrate with the rest of the family. Even when they are too old to help with the herding, they can carry out numerous other tasks such as cooking and childcare. Mongols do not have beds. Both a quick afternoon nap, like this, and a proper sleep at night are done on the floor of the *ger*.

because of the vast differences in ecological conditions across Inner Mongolia. Even the composition of the herds varies according to local conditions, with camels, for example, being common in the south and west along the Gobi, while yaks are herded only in the highlands above 2,000 metres. Suffice it to say that a well-off family in the Xilinhot region might graze herds of 200 sheep, 40 cattle, 60 horses and 3 camels. A less well-to-do family might only graze 75 sheep, 2 or 3 cattle and a horse.

Seasonal Migration

Traditionally each family was part of a larger political unit – the tribe or banner – which was, in effect, an alliance of herdsmen under the protection of a noble. In some respects the relationship between the herdsman (*arat*) and the noble (*noyon*) was feudal in nature. Like European feudalism, it was based on access to land (although for the Mongols the actual ownership of the land was immaterial – what mattered to them was the right to graze it).

The *arat* was certain routes and pasturing places, and deviations were severely punished. Grazing rights were not fixed for all time, however: as a family grew and prospered, it might gain access to more and better pastures; as it declined these pastures might be reassigned to other families. The Mongol *arat* did, however, have one advantage over the European serf: he could shift his allegiance from one *noyon* to another at will. Indeed, Genghis Khan's greatest success was the moulding of the constantly shifting alliances into a single, unitary command structure.

Since the Communist revolutions in both Inner Mongolia and the Mongolian People's Republic, the traditional nobles are no more. During the period of collectivization their role was assumed by commissars, cadres, banner leaders and other administrators. Nevertheless, the actual assignment of grazing land continued to

LEFT: Milk is one of – if not the – most important items in the Mongol diet. While men may sometimes milk mares, it is the women, known as the 'caretakers of the milk', who have the responsibility of milking the animals and making any milk-based foods such as cheese. Mare's milk is used to make a fermented – and highly potent – drink known as *kumiss*.

remain reasonably flexible. The post-Maoist reforms of China have, however, resulted in a more profound change to the system. Under the 'Reponsibility System', Mongol households now bid for the right to graze particular pastures for a designated period (fifteen, thirty or fifty years). In return for grazing rights, the family pays a specified number of animals to the State each year.

Within these social and political constraints it is the cycle of the seasons that sets the pattern of Mongol life. Mongols are, in effect, transhumant pastoralists. That is, their main migration is between summer and winter camps.

Perhaps paradoxically, the spring is the most difficult season. In the spring the Mongols move their herds out of the sheltered valleys to high ground. The pastures are at their most depleted and what little grass there is is dry and may still be covered by patches of snow. Strong winds whip up the dust and small pebbles, to the great discomfort of both man and beast. In spring the herds are in a poor state: many animals have died over the winter and even those that have survived are skinny and weak. A late snow can be catastrophic as the animals lack the strength to dig under the snow for food. Similarly, a cold spring rain can bring its own disaster: if the weather turns cold again the water can freeze. This is the reason for the Mongol saying, 'Grow in summer, fatten in fall, waste in winter, die in spring.'

The wastage is on an enormous scale: on average between five and ten million head of livestock die each year. It is a sad testimony to the rigours of life on the Mongolian steppes that each year more animals die due to the severe weather conditions than make it to market.

Summer, which runs from May to September, is considered the best season. It is a time of plenty for the Mongols as the grass is high and their livestock fatten. Mongol poetry is rich in its descriptions of summer: a recurrent image of sheep on a lush green pasture describes them as 'pearls on green velvet'. Milk production is at its highest, bringing welcome change to the spartan diet of winter. The lush grass brings some respite to the herders' migratory cycle as it enables them to stay in one place for comparatively long periods of time. Even so, some movement is necessary if the animals are not to exhaust the pasture.

The Mongol autumn is short, as the warmth of summer quickly gives way to the increasing cold of the winter. The grass is no longer lush, therefore herders must move their livestock frequently to keep them adequately fed. Moreover, they have to make sure they return to their winter camp before the weather deteriorates.

As winter approaches, the Mongols move their herds off the high pastures

RIGHT: In addition to the *mal* (the five animals of life: the horse, cattle, camel, sheep and goat), Mongols keep one other domestic animal. This is the dog. Mongol dogs are quite ferocious. They are used as watchdogs, for protecting the herds from wolves, and for hunting.

OVERLEAF
Horses have been herded on the Central Asian steppe for millennia and gave the Mongols the mobility that enabled them to conquer the largest land empire in the history of the world.

ABOVE: Here cheese is being dried on the roof of the *ger*. At other times, dung is dried on the roof to be used as fuel.

and look for sheltered valley pastures. Winter is also the time when the animals, still fat from their summer grazing, are slaughtered and their meat is dried to provision the hard months ahead.

The siting of the winter camp is of critical importance. In the other seasons there is always the option of moving on if necessary. But in severe winter conditions the choice is, quite literally, a life or death decision. If the herders get it wrong, their herds will not live to see the spring. The ideal winter camp is situated to the south of a line of hills or mountains. There is nothing mystical or superstitious about this: the mountains provide shelter from the fierce north winds. Failing that, the winter campsite may be in a small valley or basin. It goes without saying that the site must provide adequate grass for the herds to survive until spring. There must also be a water source — both for the livestock and for the family itself. Perhaps less obviously, the ideal winter location has enough of an air-flow to blow away at least some of the snow. This is essential because of the different abilities of the various animals to survive a snowfall. Horses can graze even after heavy snowfall: they use their hooves to clear away the snow so that they can get to the underlying grass. Cows and sheep, however, do not instinctively do this, which means that they must be fed by hand when snow covers the ground or else they will die of starvation. For this reason the Mongols call a winter with a heavy snowfall a 'white disaster' (*chaghan juda*). Mongols lose a huge number of their animals to white disasters. A loss of ten per cent would probably be considered acceptable, while thirty per cent losses are not uncommon. After the Xilin Gol white disaster of 1985-6, two-thirds of the livestock died off. Even this pales in comparison with the white disaster of 1977. It took ten years for some regions to bring their herd sizes back up to the level of 1976.

This is not to say, however, that all winter snowfall spells disaster for the Mongols. A light cover of snow is, in fact, beneficial as animals can eat snow to slake

their thirst. This frees them from the confines of winter pasture close to a water source, allowing them to graze further afield. Moreover, a winter without snow can be a disaster as well. These 'black disasters' (*khara juda*) may be easier on the livestock in the short term, but their effects are felt in the spring, when the lack of melting snow results in the failure of the spring grasses. This can be the last straw for livestock already weak from the winter.

Grazing

As long as herd size is in balance with the carrying capacity of the land, grazing is an efficient way to use arid and semi-arid lands. Over-grazing, however, can have severe environmental consequences. Unfortunately, over-grazing is an increasing problem in Inner Mongolia. There are several reasons for this. Today the Mongols, who are shifting from subsistence pastoralism (raising animals to supply their own needs) to commodity pastoralism (raising animals for profit), are under pressure from the government to produce ever more meat and wool for both the national and the world markets. This has resulted in an increasing number of animals being herded in Inner Mongolia (since 1949 the number of animals has increased by more than 300 per cent). The situation is further exacerbated by the fact that Han immigrants in Inner Mongolia are taking up livestock raising. Lacking a pastoral tradition, the Han do not have the skills to graze their animals properly. For the most part, the Han continue to live in towns and villages. They are 9-to-5 pastoralists, as it were, driving their animals out into the countryside during the day and bringing them back to town each night. The concentration of so many animals grazing within only a few hours' walk from town has resulted in the complete denudation of all vegetative matter around many towns and villages in Inner Mongolia.

The amount of land available for pasture is shrinking in other ways as well. The extension of irrigation, the development of fast-ripening strains of grain, the

ABOVE: Even the most recalcitrant mare must be brought in for milking. The long mane of this mare provides a convenient handle for bringing her back to the camp.

ABOVE: Curiously acupuncture, a traditional medicine invented by the Chinese, is also used by the Mongols on their horses.

artificial lengthening of the agricultural season by growing crops under plastic and other developments have resulted in ever more pasture land being turned over to agricultural production. The net result of all this is that each year there is less (and worse) land available for the herds. This has the effect of concentrating more and more animals on less and less land. Over-concentration invariably leads to the exhaustion of the land and the destruction of the pastures. It comes as no surprise that Inner Mongolia suffers from some of the worst desertification in the world today.

Dwellings

The basic dwelling of the Mongol is the yurt or, more properly, the *ger*, the basic design of which was developed in antiquity and has remained unchanged for more than a millennium. Even today, as the inhabitants of Inner Mongolia move into permanent brick and adobe houses for their winter quarters, the *ger* remains the mainstay of their migratory existence.

*Ger*s come in several sizes, but their shape is always the same: a circular tent surmounted by a conical roof. The walls of the *ger* are made of a frame of birch willows woven into a collapsible lattice held together by leather strips. Each section of lattice (called a *khana*) is approximately 2 metres high and 2 to 2½ metres long. Sections of lattice are joined together to form a circle.

The willow lattice is covered by layers of felt held in place by ropes. The stringing of these ropes has a symbolic aspect: they are strung in a manner that replicates the sun's rotation. The number of layers of felt varies: in summer the walls will be just one layer thick; in winter three layers will be used. Rich Mongols cover the whole *ger* in canvas or plastic to provide additional protection from rain.

The roof of the *ger* is also made of felt supported by willow poles. In all but the smallest *ger* a centre pole is erected. Smaller poles radiate out from it (rather like the spokes of a parasol) to the top of the *khana*. As with the walls, the roof can be

BELOW: Instead of a Western-style lasso, Mongol herdsmen carry a long, flexible pole with a rope loop on one end. The loop is dropped over the head of the horse that the herdsman wants to separate from the rest of the herd – a technique requiring great dexterity and horsemanship.

covered with as many layers of felt as conditions require – fewer in summer, more in winter. The roofcloths can be folded back to let in light and air when the weather is good or completely sealed when it is bad.

Each *ger* has a wooden door that can be covered with a cloth flap in bad weather. The *ger* also has a smoke-hole (*öröke*) in the centre of the roof. This hole can be up to one metre in diameter and can also be covered with a flap in inclement weather. While there are no windows, the felt covering the *khana* can be raised or folded up in order to provide ventilation in warm weather. In winter, dirt or wood is placed on the lower edge of the *khana* wall covering to provide an extra weather seal.

The floor of the *ger* is covered in several layers. Animal hides are laid on the ground, providing a layer of insulation. A layer of old felt is placed on top of the hides and a layer of new felt is placed on top of the old. Finally, any rugs that the family may have are laid out. Rich Mongols will even have portable wooden floors.

In the middle of the floor stands the hearth. This is a metal container approximately half a metre in diameter made of iron bands supported on four or six feet. The hearth stands on a rectangle of bare earth in the centre of the *ger*. As wood is extremely scarce on the steppes, the traditional fuel is dried dung.

A family usually travels with more than one *ger*. The common campsite arrangement is to have two or three *ger*s laid out in a line. Each *ger* is oriented so that its door faces the south-east (both as a protection from the prevailing winds and as a holdover from the shamanistic worship of the sun). The largest *ger* serves as the main living area, both as a day-room and for sleeping. The family uses a smaller *ger* as their kitchen and store-room. It takes about twenty minutes to assemble a *ger* and about twice that to take it down and pack it.

Diet

The staples of the Mongol diet are, of course, meat and milk. The main food animal is the sheep, although cattle are also eaten, and the main forms of cooking are boiling and roasting. Sheep are never eaten young, however – the notion of eating lamb is anathema to the herdsman.

Mongols slaughter their sheep in two ways. One is the slit-throat method common the world over. The other method, however, is peculiar to the Mongols. In this method the animal is laid on its back and a small slit is made under the rib cage. The slaughterer then reaches through the slit and with his hand breaks the cardiac artery. Death is quick and very clean. No blood is spilled at all as it drains directly into the chest cavity.

Milk and milk products are important parts of the Mongol diet and all five of the herd animals are milked. Sheep and cattle provide the main sources of milk, although camels and goats are milked in times of hardship. In terms of quantity, milk from horses falls far behind sheep and cattle, but it is nonetheless important. A great delicacy is mare's milk which is drunk in a fermented and intoxicating form called *kumiss*. To make *kumiss*, mare's milk is put into a pouch which is hung in the *ger*. Every time anyone passes the pouch they give it a shake or a stir. A draught may be taken out at any time, and the pouch is constantly replenished by milk from the latest milking. One result of this is that the strength of the liquor varies from day to day and from *ger* to *ger*. Strong *kumiss*, which is a cloudy but refreshing drink, can pack quite a kick. Indeed, the Mongols consume most milk products in the fermented state. Thus neither cow's nor sheep's milk is customarily drunk fresh; more commonly they are made into a liquid yogurt.

Fermented milk in general is called *esüg*, but it may take a great many varieties. Cow's milk, for example, can be made into *taragh* (a sour milk not unlike thin yogurt), *arkhi* (a slightly smoky distilled spirit), *besleg* (an extremely tough cheese), *orum* (a solid cream) and *tos* (butter, a modern innovation), to name but a few. In summer it is common to see solid cream in trays or long strips of cheese laid out on the roof of the *ger* drying in the sun.

As with so many other aspects of their lives, there is a seasonal aspect to the

LEFT: Even in his old age, this man still travels with his son's family on their annual migratory cycle. When he is too old to ride on horseback, he will make the migration in the same cart that carries the *ger* and all the other family possessions.

Mongol diet. Traditionally more meat than milk (and milk products) is eaten in the winter and more milk (and milk products) than meat in the summer. This is due in part to the availability of milk (which is more abundant when the summer grass is high). But other factors also come into play. The Mongols kill off part of their herds each autumn and winter, both to relieve pressure on grazing land and to cull those animals that would not survive the rigours of winter. Meat is also easier to preserve in the naturally low temperatures of winter. As a result meat is seldom eaten fresh (except on ceremonial or feast days). Instead meat from the slaughtered animals is dried for future use. The dried strips are soaked for several hours before being cooked (even then the meat is extremely tough when served). A common dish is a thick soup made from boiled meat into which a handful of toasted millet (or, more extravagantly, rice) is thrown.

Unlike the Chinese and the Russians, the Mongols drink tea with milk. Tea, water and milk are placed in a big pot in which they are all boiled together. Salt is also added to the beverage, which is called *suuteichai*. For breakfast or lunch a handful of toasted millet may be added to the concoction. To round out breakfast and lunch the Mongols may eat *öröm* or *khuruud* (milk curd or cheese) and any cold boiled mutton left over from the previous day. The evening meal is the main meal of the day. Even then the food is quite basic. The most common dishes are pieces of boiled mutton mixed with noodles and meat soup mixed with millet. Vegetables are rare at the best of times, and are non-existent for weeks on end. As the Mongols do not grow vegetables, they rely on trade with townspeople for their greens. The most common vegetable in the Mongol diet is pickled cabbage.

Nadam

Nadam means 'games' – specifically the three 'manly' games of archery, wrestling and horsemanship. These sports of might and military strength date back to the times of the forefathers of Genghis Khan. Traditionally every occasion (from weddings to national holidays) that brought together groups of Mongols was accompa-

BELOW: The central characteristic of the steppe is that it is a vast, featureless plain. The lack of trees is behind the Mongol saying, 'If you want to hang yourself, you have to walk for 100 miles'. Almost the only vegetation is grass, which is what makes the steppe so valuable as grazing land. However, over-grazing is a serious environmental problem in Inner Mongolia today.

nied by racing, wrestling and archery competitions. Small *nadam*s might last just a few hours, but large *nadam*s can go on for days. As with so much in Mongol life, there is a seasonal aspect to the *nadam*s. They most often take place towards the end of summer, when the lush grass will support the coming together of many families and when fat beasts and milk are plentiful.

Since the Cultural Revolution began, *nadam*s have been strictly controlled by the Chinese authorities who continue to fear Mongol nationalism and seek to avoid Tibetan-style confrontations. While small, local, *nadam*s were sometimes allowed, large festivals were prohibited. This has been relaxed slightly in recent years, but only at a cost. The *nadam*, like so much of Mongol life and culture, is being taken over by the Chinese. For example, although the *nadam* shown on pages 116-23 conformed in some ways to the traditional pattern, it began with a large parade that included the military, groups of police, workers and cadres; and awards were given for model workers of the state. There was nothing Mongol about it: it was a statement of Chinese power.

The *nadam* proper consists of a number of sporting events. There are several classes of racing and horsemanship. Most important is a long (30-kilometre or more) horse race for mature horses over six years old. These horses are ridden by boys or girls between the ages of eight and fifteen, the idea being that the jockey must be strong enough to guide the horse but not restrict its willingness or 'heart'. Traditionally the Mongols have always been more interested in stamina than in sprinting, as this race shows. Children ride without saddles or stirrups so that if they fall off they won't catch their feet in some part of the tackle and be dragged by the running horse. Since Mongols begin to ride as soon as they can walk, the ability to ride 30-odd kilometres, for either a boy or girl, is considered no great feat.

The wrestling contest begins with the massed wrestlers (often 100 or more) dancing into the competition field in their distinctive dress. The wrestlers dance to the music of Buddhist chants in great, swooping bird-like movements. They

ABOVE: Sheep are the primary source of meat in the Mongols' diet. They are also the most important source of wool, which is used both domestically by the herding families themselves and as their most important 'cash crop'. Sheep are shorn once – and sometimes twice – a year. Mongol herdsmen produce much of China's wool, and China is now third in world production of wool.

RIGHT: Today the component parts of a *ger* can be bought ready-made. In the centre of the photograph, at the back of the display, are the *khana* – collapsible sections of birch willow lattice which are joined together in a circle to form the walls of the *ger*. On the right is the wheel which is placed on top of the centre pole in the *ger* to form the conical-shaped roof. Poles (*left*) radiate out from this to the top of the *khana*.

The *Nadam*

Nadam means 'games' – the manly games of archery, wrestling and horsemanship – and were a traditional part of any occasion or festivity that brought Mongols together. The traditional *nadam* was related to a festival for fertility and Buddhist worship and was a chance for families, banners and leagues to get together and compete in tests of strength and skill.

Nowadays the *nadam*, like so much of Mongol life and culture, is being taken over by the Chinese. The *nadam* on these pages was to celebrate the fact that, according to official statistics, Xilin Gol League had produced 10 million head of livestock. It also coincided, whether by accident or design, with the first free elections in the Mongolian People's Republic just across the border.

LEFT: Mare's milk and a gift of cloth are the traditional Mongol symbol of welcome and hospitality. Mare's milk is carried at the head of the procession that begins the *nadam*.

BELOW: A massed display of dancing at the *nadam*.

ABOVE: Mongol wrestling is rather like Japanese sumo wrestling. The winner is the one who forces the other to touch the ground with any part of the body except the sole of the foot. Traditionally, two evenly matched contenders could struggle motionlessly for many minutes. Now, however, the Chinese have imposed a 40-minute time limit: if one man has not won in that time, the winner is decided by the flip of a coin.

LEFT: The most important horse race is over 35 kilometres for horses over six years old. The horses are ridden by boys or girls between the ages of eight and fifteen; the jockey must be strong enough to guide the horse but not restrict its willingness of heart.

then divide into two groups and competition begins. The wrestlers all fight their opponents at the same time, with the winners of each 'round' then pairing off again to begin the next round.

Traditional Mongolian wrestling is akin to Japanese sumo wrestling. It is a competition between two opponents who try to knock each other to the ground. The wrestlers grasp each other on the arm or by the back of each other's jackets and kick at each other. These kicks must be side swipes rather than direct kicks at the shin and the winner is the one who forces the other to touch the ground with any part of the body except the sole of the foot. The importance of control and balance can make the matches vary enormously in duration. A quick flip can end the match in seconds, while two evenly matched contenders may struggle motionlessly for many minutes. The official *nadam* now imposes a time limit of 40 minutes and (in a Chinese innovation) if one man has not won in that time, the winner is decided by the toss of a coin. Mongols are upset by this ruling, which they say distorts the idea of the game. Although the main wrestling competition is for men, there can be boys' and women's events as well.

The other important event is archery. Like wrestling, there are separate competitions for men and women. Competition can take several forms, including shooting at stationary targets and shooting from a moving horse.

Religion

Mongol religion is traditionally shamanistic, but because of their world conquest Mongols came into contact with many of the world's great religions. Contrary to the behaviour of most conquerors, the Mongols did not put other religions to the sword. Indeed, they themselves frequently adopted the religion of the peoples they conquered. Thus Mongols in China adopted Tibetan (lamaist) Buddhism, while the Mongols in Persia and the lands of the Golden Horde embraced Islam. There have even been Nestorian Christian Mongols. At the same time, they kept some of their older, shamanistic, practices. This is especially true in Inner Mongolia, where shamanistic practices continue to this day.

The ancient shamanistic religion of the Mongols has its foundations in the spirits of the land, the sky, ancestors and animals. Shamans were religious specialists who served as intermediaries between the spirits and the living people. Mongols make their shamanistic offerings and sacrifice to increase fertility (both their own and their herds) before an *oboo*, a pile of stones that serves as an outdoor altar.

LEFT: Mongolian women in traditional costume are flanked by soldiers of the Chinese Red Army at the most important *nadam* to be held in Inner Mongolia for almost a decade. The Red Army is a constant presence throughout Inner Mongolia, underlying both China's fear of invasion from the north and the extent of the Chinese domination of Mongolia.

RIGHT: This identification badge is worn by a representative of one of the banners taking part in the *nadam*, and sets out his name, banner and commune. It is written in both Chinese characters and Mongolian script.
During the Cultural Revolution in China, the teaching of the Mongolian language was prohibited. Recent years have seen some relaxation of restriction. However, there is no higher education teaching in the Mongolian language in China, and all good jobs and government positions depend on a knowledge of Chinese. As a result, many of the best and brightest young Mongols are being indirectly weaned away from their own language and culture.

OVERLEAF
Mongol and Chinese officials from the various banners and district and administrative offices watching the *nadam*.

ABOVE: The design and pattern on the wrestler's trousers are also peculiar to each individual banner.

Mongolian costume

A distinctive feature of Mongolian culture are the traditional costumes which, even after years of Communist domination, survive in both Inner and Outer Mongolia. Normally, Mongol clothes are very plain. Their robes tend to be a single, dark colour tied with a sash of a contrasting colour. On special occasions such as a *nadam* or wedding, special, highly decorated clothes are worn. Often these clothes are decorated with intricate metalwork patterns.

LEFT: Headdresses such as this are now rare and worn only for a *nadam* and other special occasions. This one shows a mixture of Chinese and Mongolian styles.

ABOVE: Western influences, too, are beginning to make their mark.

During a ritual, a pole or spear is stuck into the *oboo* and coloured banners are hung from it. *Oboo*s, often decorated with pictures of horses, are still a common sight in Inner Mongolia. Even today, many Mongols have *oboo*s, outside their homes.

Some Mongols have shrines in their homes, often now with a picture of Genghis Khan who is considered a personal representation of the sky. Statues of the five animals of life, the horse, cattle, camel, sheep and goat, stand in front of the picture. When the family receives a special gift of food they leave it before the Khan for him to eat before they touch it themselves. Offerings are also burnt on this altar. The altar is always placed in the back left side of the *ger* facing the door (the same place as a Buddhist altar is placed). This is the most respected space in the *ger* and is where special guests or respected older people are urged to sit.

Sedentarization

Since 1949, the Chinese government has actively encouraged a policy of northern migration, both to relieve chronic population pressure in China proper and to consolidate Chinese political and military control over the region. Mongols are now a minority in their own country. Moreover, Chinese control the government and education, and fill virtually all positions of power.

The extension of agriculture in the region (made possible by the building of irrigation works and the development of fast-maturing seeds) has had an even more direct effect on the Mongols. Each hectare of land converted to agriculture means one less hectare of land for pasture. Further complicating the situation is the fact that the Mongols are simultaneously under government pressure to produce more and more livestock for the State. This is, of course, a recipe for environmental disaster.

Traditional Mongol migration patterns have been severely disrupted by the incoming Han. Not only have they been denied access to some of the best grazing land as it has been converted to agricultural use, but the collectivization and communization plans implemented in the 1950s and 1960s have taken their toll. Recently the old collectives and communes have been dismantled by the post-Maoist privatization schemes of Deng Xiaoping, yet privatization has created new pressures on the herders. Under the Responsibility System individual families now contract for the right to graze specific plots of land. Rights to *kulum*s (essentially 'homesteads' or 'enclosures') are granted for reasonably long periods of time (up to fifty years in some cases) in return for an annual payment. Certain conditions must be met, however, for the contract to be maintained. Thus, for example, the herder may be required to 'improve' the land by building a brick/adobe home on the land and to sink a well. Moreover, while the *kulum*s can be quite large (*kulum*s of thirty or more square kilometres are not uncommon), they are still small compared with the extent of range formerly covered in the family's annual migration cycle. Few such parcels of land are big enough to contain both adequate summer and winter pastures. Because the contracting family no longer migrates over great distances, there is an increasing tendency to use their 'improved' house as a more or less permanent base camp. A further consequence of raising livestock on a restricted grazing base is that the herders are increasingly reliant on stored fodder (rather than open grazing land) to feed their livestock over winter. This has the effect of increasing the Mongols' involvement with agriculture. Thus the formerly nomadic pastoralists are gradually becoming only semi-nomadic, or even sedentary, pastoralists. Together these changes conspire to tie the herder to one place. Such creeping sedentarization may well sound the death knell for the Mongols' nomadic existence.

LEFT: Buddhist monks at prayer in Xilinhot, the headquarters town of the Xilin Gol League. Religion in China was brutally suppressed during the Cultural Revolution, and this is the only surviving monastery in the town. Although the Mongol religion was traditionally shamanistic, the Mongols frequently adopted the religion of the peoples they conquered, while at the same time keeping some of their older shamanistic practices.

125

THE
REINDEER
HERDERS
OF SIBERIA

DR PIERS VITEBSKY

In the Siberian Arctic, where winter temperatures fall as low as minus 70 degrees Celsius, live the Eveny, a little-known group of reindeer herders whose lives revolve around their animals' annual migration patterns. Settled agriculture is impossible in this climate. Decades of enforced collectivization have drastically undermined their culture and family life; under perestroika *the Eveny are demanding a return to partial nomadism to restore these.*

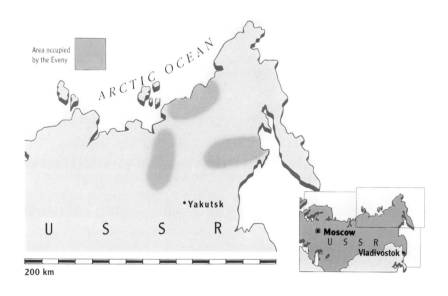

Area occupied by the Eveny

ARCTIC OCEAN

• Yakutsk

U S S R

■ Moscow
U S S R
Vladivostok •

200 km

LEFT: An Even reindeer herder. Herding used to be a family activity, but now women and children are almost entirely absent. The majority of men, especially the younger ones, live a bachelor existence. Now, in April, the sun is high and the weather comparatively mild.

I
T IS LATE WINTER and the temperature is minus 40 degrees Celsius. All morning one group of reindeer herders has been waiting on a windswept hilltop, scanning the surrounding slopes with binoculars and picking out the shape of their colleagues several kilometres away. Mounted on reindeer, the men in the distance weave their way through the bare, feather-thin larch trunks which seem drawn with black ink against the overcast white ground. They have found part of the herd and are driving it towards the waiting men. At last, the sound of reindeer grunting and men whistling can be heard. The first deer filter between the nearest trees, the camouflage of their fur blending closely with the snow and the trees' rough, grey-brown, bark. Suddenly the waiting men burst into action with their lassos, singling out deer, controlling, separating them. For several days they have been felling larches and constructing fencing in order to provide enclosures in which the pregnant females can be separated from the rest of the herd. By the end of the day nearly 2,000 reindeer will be swirling in a tightly-packed mass around the finished corral and the herders will sleep to the sound of their ceaseless grunting and drumming of hooves.

These are some of the 'nomadic' reindeer herders of the Siberian Arctic. How has nomadism fared under sixty years of Communism, and how is it now being transformed yet again under *perestroika*?

The Eveny (pronounced Evény, singular: Evén) number about 17,000 and are scattered in small communities across thousands of square kilometres, interspersed and mixed with settlements of other ethnic groups. Like their cousins the Evenk, they speak a Tungus language which suggests an origin in Manchuria in northeastern China, far to the south. The Eveny are just one of 26 'small peoples' of Siberia and the Soviet North, who include the Chukchi, the Khanty, the Mansy, the Nenets, the Nganasan, the Eskimo, and many more. Today numbering little more than 180,000 in all, these peoples are the original inhabitants whom Russian adventurers and fur traders met in the seventeenth century as they pushed eastwards across the Urals to the Pacific coast of what is now the USSR. The Russians' use of firearms made this encounter an uneven one, and all the native groups were sooner or later incorporated into the expanding Russian empire.

Because of the extremely short summers and the long, hard winters there could be no settled agriculture in this area. Animal populations themselves migrated, and the tiny human populations followed the animals. Some lived by hunting the elk, wild reindeer and the many smaller animals of the northern inland forests. Others, on the coast, hunted walrus, seals and whales. Fishing was also important throughout the area.

The Russians came originally in quest of furs. Since the Revolution in 1917, Russian settlement has increased enormously. Much of this is for the exploitation of oil, gas and other minerals and is almost entirely concentrated in towns. Workers from the European part of the USSR bring their technical skills to the North both out of idealism and because they are attracted by wage increments which are graduated according to the hardship of the area. The native peoples remain relatively uninvolved in these activities and rely instead on the modern development of their traditional occupations of hunting, fishing and reindeer herding – though in some areas mineral exploitation poses a serious threat to these. All these peoples are considered vulnerable and have been the subject of special protective policies throughout the Soviet period – though, as we shall see, these policies are now widely judged to have been unsuccessful.

Siberia occupies most of the USSR east of the Urals and amounts to roughly 10 per cent of the Earth's land area. The Eveny live in the most rugged part of Siberia. This landscape is vast. In some areas the mountains rise to over 2,000 metres and in the still calm of winter hold within them the deep frosts of what is the coldest area in the entire northern hemisphere, with temperatures dropping to minus 70 degrees Celsius. The short summers are often hot, but since the ground below the surface

RIGHT: The Eveny live in the most rugged part of Siberia. This is the coldest area in the northern hemisphere: winter temperatures can fall to minus 70 degrees Celsius and the ground below the surface never thaws.

In some places the mountains rise to nearly 2,000 metres. Larch trees cover the lower slopes, growing mostly on south-facing slopes and in sheltered gullies. On some north-facing slopes, ice-caps can remain throughout the short, hot summer. Along the rivers grow willows and rose-hips. In early autumn much of the forest floor is covered with mushrooms, which the reindeer love. In the winter, most vegetation dies down and the deer must scrape for lichen with their hooves and antlers.

never thaws, melting groundwater drains badly. Then the steepest mountain slopes are often boggy and the countryside swarms with mosquitos.

In winter, herders travel for hours at a time on sledges up and down the steep icy slopes of rivers, littered with huge turquoise slabs of buckled ice. In the short summer and the golden autumn, these rivers flow fast and the colour of the larch trees throws into vivid relief the burnt-out areas left by forest fires, dated by their new growth and linked to people's own lifespans. The cold and damp cause severe health problems and there is a high death rate from accidents, particularly as the ice breaks up in rivers and lakes in early summer. In emergency, helicopters can be summoned by radio. But this is possible only if weather permits, and people die for lack of medical attention because they cannot be reached.

Over this immense and dangerous landscape people often work and travel alone, in an atmosphere of independence and self-reliance. Numerous places suitable for a night halt contain a little iron stove and a stack of ready-cut poles on which one has only to hang one's own canvas. Caches of equipment and provisions are stockpiled for wayfarers in unlocked huts or on tree-platforms. In any human shelter, the focal point is the stove. Though the traditional shamans, or spirit-mediums, have largely died out, everyone still respects the spirit which is believed to reside in the fire. This spirit must be fed with the first portion of any meal and especially of any alcohol, before humans can eat or drink. In particular it will not allow a newcomer to sleep easily until he has fed it himself.

The reform of nomadism under Soviet rule

Reindeer herding is the mainstay of the economy across much of the Soviet North. As a system of production, it depends on an intimate knowledge of one's animals and of their interaction with the landscape across which they move. It uses a special vocabulary of reindeer markings, behaviour and moods, and it requires unceasing teamwork from before dawn till after dark among a handful of people who may see nobody but each other for weeks or months on end. The work of the reindeer herder cannot be separated from a whole way of life and its culture.

BELOW: Throughout the territory are caches of equipment and provisions which the herders can use as they follow the reindeer on their migration routes. In this photograph canvas is being hung over ready-cut poles to form a tent. This will be the herders' home until the reindeer have moved on too far for them to be able to remain in this camp. To put up a tent, the herders shovel away the snow and then tie the poles together so that they balance on the frozen ground without the assistance of guy-ropes.

This culture is essentially nomadic. At such low temperatures, the vegetation on which the reindeer graze grows back very slowly. In order to avoid overgrazing, each herd must move constantly over an annual cycle of several hundred kilometres. Under these conditions, which are far tougher than in Scandinavia, each reindeer requires around sixty hectares of pasture. Even culture is thus a culture adjusted to vast spaces. For example, until the advent of written messages and later radio, appointments to meet up would be made a year in advance and people would leave messages to show where they had gone by bending a twig or arranging stones on the ground. Many of life's necessities are made from skins, antlers and other animal products, as well as from larch trees. Though they use manufactured clothes in the summer, the Eveny regard the only reliable winter clothing as that which they have made themselves from reindeer skins. Their woman cut up hide of different colours and inlay these in distinctive patterns for each group. A high value is placed on hospitality: a visitor arriving at any hour of the day or night is immediately fed, and under a custom called *nimat*, a hunter is obliged to give an animal he has killed to someone else, who then distributes the meat.

Yet it is precisely this nomadic herding culture which has clashed with the Soviet authorities since the advent of Communist rule. From the 1930s onwards, official policy has aimed to weaken or eliminate nomadism, which was considered 'backward'. Before the Soviet period there were no villages or concentrations of population. The people were organized into intermarrying clans, each clan with its own territory over which it migrated. Families scattered to survive the winter and came together for the spring and summer to graze their deer together and enjoy social life in fishing camps along the rivers and lakes. In an attempt to remove the supposed unfairness of the pre-revolutionary Russian empire, which included a small number of big herd-owners, the state took over the herds and created 'collective', state-owned herds. Herders then became employees of the state, with guaranteed wages. The need to administer this, combined with the wish to provide better schooling and medical facilities, led to the establishment of villages, each of which

LEFT: There are normally up to half a dozen tents in an encampment. The herders' few material needs are transported by reindeer sled. Several pairs of deer are harnessed together in a caravan, with one or two spares at the back which also act as a brake when going downhill. Travellers usually carry a full set of tools and equipment, since they can never be sure they will not be caught by bad weather without shelter for the night.

RIGHT: The main food in the camp is reindeer meat, with some meat of wild animals and, in the autumn, berries. The herders also eat bread brought from the village, or sometimes bake their own from flour. Flour is flown in to the North from other agricultural regions, as are tins of milk, jam, and other luxuries. The Eveny eat meat by holding a large piece in their teeth and cutting off a piece upwards with a sharp knife.

was intended to act as the focal point for the surrounding herders. A typical village may have a population of one or two thousand, and control an area of perhaps one million hectares.

Since the 1960s, if not earlier, herding can best be called semi-nomadic. The animals and the herders who look after them move around in nomadic camps. But the society as a whole is largely settled, and the herders look towards the village not only for their administration but also for their social and family life. Some of the customs most closely associated with the nomadic way of life have now disappeared. The distinctive Even circle dances survive only in village folklore troupes, as does the heavily costumed dance of the shaman. The winter clothing of the Eveny is increasinly being made in workshops in the village, rather than in family tents out in the herding camps.

Though there is much local variation, each of these villages is organized as a total 'state farm' (*sovkhoz*), which provides the villagers' employment. The Soviet Union is a multi-ethnic society and these villages may contain people of many different nationalities besides the Eveny, who may not always even be in a majority. There will usually be Yakut horse specialists, Russian engineers and technicians, and a few Lithuanians or Buryats. Some of these outsiders may be former exiles to Siberia who have stayed on and now work as bookkeepers or odd-job men. But unlike the situation of many other northern native peoples, administrative and Party positions are often held by Eveny themselves. A typical village is built of substantial wooden houses and contains administrative offices, the community hall, kindergarten, school, hospital, stores, airstrip, cattle and fur farm, veterinary facilities and slaughterhouse (village offices of the Communist Party are now beginning to disappear). Outside, anywhere between 70 and 300 kilometres away across a vast landscape, are sprinkled a dozen or so reindeer-herders' camps. Though tents used to be covered with reindeer hide, now they are usually made of canvas. Each camp contains a 'brigade' of six or seven herders and a few dependent relatives or other helpers. Each also has a salaried female 'tentkeeper', often a pensioner, who cooks for the working herders.

The growing crisis in family life

Female tentkeepers are needed in the camps because herding is in a deep demographic crisis: there has been an alarming decay of family life as fewer and fewer young people come out from the village to work as herders. Reindeer herding

PREVIOUS PAGE:
The reindeer are constantly on the move in search of food. Here, in the April sunshine, they are at their thinnest after the long, hard winter.

LEFT: Herders always camp near a river or lake. Between October and May, they have to quarry their water like rock and transport it by sledge. In this climate tea is a great comfort and the herders will drink it when they come in from the cold and again to fortify themselves before returning outside.

RIGHT: The block of ice is split cleanly with a blow of a knife or axe. Once it is simmering on the stove inside, it will crackle as it continues to split before melting down. A great deal of wood is needed to boil a large cauldron of water. This man is married, though his wife lives far away in the village. Throughout the Soviet Union, wedding rings are worn on the right hand.

The spring round-up

This is one of the main spring corrals. The main problem of managing a herd is that the animals must continually be dispersed to graze and bunched again to prevent their getting lost. Corraling allows the health, weight and condition to be checked and makes it possible for them to be sorted into separate pens for different pastoral regimes. Here, soon before the calving season, the pregnant does are separated from the rest of the herd for special attention. Deer will not be kept in the corral for more than one or two days, as they dislike being crowded and are unable to graze. This is a period of hard work for the herders, who will often work very actively from before dawn until after dark.

BELOW: Reindeer are not ridden in Scandinavia, but in Siberia they are considered to give the greatest mobility and manoeuvrability. In addition, reindeer will allow a mounted man to move among them much more freely than a man on foot.

ABOVE: Lassos are made of plaited reindeer hide and thrown with extreme accuracy around the antlers of a deer which is to be separated from the main herd.

ABOVE: Each April, the deer and the herders reach the same point in their annual cycle of migrations. The fencing behind the men took weeks to build and is then repaired every year in readiness for the corral. Sometimes a migration route has to be changed slightly to match new circumstances of vegetation and microclimate, and then an old corral must be abandoned and a new one built.

amounts to virtually the entire economy of much of the Soviet native North, but only a small proportion of the population is involved in this occupation. Herding used to be a family activity, but now women and children are almost entirely absent. The majority of men, especially the younger ones, live a bachelor existence. Even those who are married, usually older men, rarely see their wives and children.

It is not simply that the women prefer the comforts of TV and village life. The main reason is their desire to be near their children, who are obliged to stay in the village to attend school. These women work in the growing service sector as schoolteachers, storekeepers and accountants, jobs which allow them to look after a house in the village. They know that those children who do not have a close relative in the village stay in the boarding school. This is an institution which is widespread in the Soviet North but which has become the focus of complaints in newspapers, where native adults write of the torments inflicted on them in their own lives by their enforced separation from their own parents. Certainly, boarding school is no substitute for a parent's love. But in addition, schools generally use the Russian language and a curriculum far removed from the realities of herding. They are widely blamed for blocking the transmission of native culture between generations who have become virtual strangers to each other.

How could such a situation have arisen? There is a contradiction, still unresolved, at the heart of collectivization. Before the 1930s, each nomadic clan had its own territory, as their families and reindeer moved constantly with the seasons in search of pasture. The policy of collectivization was originally conceived to bring about the socialist transformation of the agrarian society of the European part of the USSR. It was then applied without appropriate adjustments to nomadic herders who, like the peasants, often resisted fiercely. Here, it had at least two additional aims. The first was to 'rationalize' herding, with the result that the numbers of deer kept and the dates and locations of migration are now laid down by veterinary specialists and botanists; the second was to 'civilize' the people, a worldwide response of governments when faced with nomads, by settling them in centralized villages, providing services and educating their children there. Yet the reindeer and their herders still needed to keep constantly on the move. As a result, the old form of nomadism as a way of life, in which the whole family migrated together, was condemned and eliminated; the present system, in which looking after reindeer was isolated from its social base, effectively reduced it to a worker's job like any other.

Yet the cost to family life has been high and it now threatens the continuation of herding altogether. Herding is no ordinary nine-to-five job. Controlling the movement of the herd requires skilled judgement and constant attention every day of the year, often from dawn to dusk and even throughout the night. The animals have to be kept constantly on the move without being allowed to scatter out of control. At roughly two-month intervals, the herders pack up their entire camp and migrate some 50 to 100 kilometres to keep up with the movement of the herd. The skills of herding include an understanding not only of pasture and the animals' nutritional needs, but also of their psychology. A few of the best deer are kept near the camp and milked, or, if male, castrated and trained as riding deer or sledge pullers. These domestic deer have names and people say that they must be offered salt to lick from an outstretched palm every time they are called or the deer will feel cheated and

LEFT: Inside a corral the deer always swirl anticlockwise. The deer which have been allowed to keep their antlers until the spring are mostly females, who need them in order to scrape the snow off the pasture for their young. Most of the male deer are without antlers since these were sawn off in the previous autumn in order to prevent the animals from injuring each other in fights during the rutting season.

become uncooperative. Domestic deer are never lassoed. The reindeer of the main herd, however, are still half wild and it is a rare herder who knows all his 2,000 deer by sight and personal history. Even inside a corral, these animals can be captured only with the aid of a lasso. Strategies of herding involve both deferring to this timidity and taking advantage of it. The animals respond to wind direction and smell. They will tolerate the smooth, easy movement among them of a mounted herder where they would not tolerate him if he were on foot. They like clear ground and avoid obstructions, especially those which resemble a human figure. The herd can be driven away by men flapping their arms and shouting, or channelled forward by elaborate arrangements of decoys and fences.

A way of life like this must be learned from early childhood. Life in the village school is no substitute for constant first-hand experience of the subtleties and intricacies of reindeer herding and the development of a close understanding between humans and animals. Herders insist that only people who have this experience from childhood can grow into skilled herders. The reason for the growing elderliness of the herding profession is not only the gulf between the standard of comfort in the village and the tents, but also the simple fact that few young people any longer have sufficient knowledge or familiarity with reindeer.

Within the herding camps, both men and women are able to do any job and there are still a few young women who are superb herders until they have children and withdraw to the village. But the general absence of women has skewed the distribution of male and female roles. The men's lives have something of the atmosphere of a barracks, while the female tentkeeper often has to perform basic housekeeping tasks for everyone, using her tent as a communal canteen. Above all, this entails cooking meat several times a day and keeping a constant supply of tea available. Her own herders or visiting travellers may suddenly appear at any moment, exhausted from many hours of strenuous activity in the bitter cold. She also milks the domestic deer, cures skins and spreads fresh larch fronds regularly on the tent floors as a fragrant carpet. Meanwhile, the men spend much time out and about, herding, chasing, bunching, and separating deer across huge distances. Often they have to bed down for the night far from the camp, using a makeshift tent or one of the little huts where supplies are stored at various locations. However strongly built, these long-awaited huts sometimes turn out to have been wrecked by bears who have raided them for food and scattered their supplies of flour, butter and sugar.

Family life and the cycle of the seasons

In late June, the village school closes for the summer holidays and the children are at last free to come to the camp with their mothers. Except for short periods of leave in the village, this is the only time when the herding profession can enjoy a normal family life. In practice, only those children come whose fathers or other close relatives are herders. This may amount to only one in ten of the children. The remainder may never see a camp, or even ride reindeer, throughout their childhood. For those children who do go, the summer is a time of tranquillity and intimacy. They pick flowers and berries, help with fetching and chopping wood, and learn to handle reindeer through the easy familiarity of daily contact and the sense of being useful. There is a striking contrast between the children who appear shy and awkward in school but who are clearly strong and confident in the camps, and capable of meeting any demand put on them.

On 1 September, school begins again. Helicopters fetch the children from the camps, or, if low cloud prevents this, the children must be escorted back on reindeer caravans. Most if not all of the women go too, and the mood of the camp changes back to the quiet dullness of bachelor routine. The pace of work remains hard. Just as the men must migrate every few weeks, so their yearly routine is punctuated with periodic corrals. This time the corral is part of the great autumn round-up and slaughter. During the summer, groups of deer have moved far and wide in search of food. Just a few weeks ago, in early autumn, the advent of mushrooms

RIGHT: An Even toddler bundled up against the bitter cold. The Eveny's outer clothing is made mostly of reindeer fur, which is extremely heat-retentive because each individual hair is hollow. The beadwork of the adult echoes a style of decoration found throughout much of the Arctic from Alaska to Greenland. The scarves with silver and gold threads are from India and are popular throughout the Soviet Union.

RIGHT: A crowd of spectators and competitors at the spring festival and games. Each village, or state farm, must enter a team for each event, on pain of a fine. The people gathered here are not only Eveny, but also Chukchi and Yukaghir, the other 'small peoples' of the northern Yakut Republic. Note the inlaid space rocket draped over the back of the reindeer in the lower centre. Each village has its own distinctive pattern of inlaying white fur on brown. The banner which is partly visible in the lower left is of the state farm from Momsky Region.

OVERLEAF:
The highlight of the spring festival is the reindeer racing, both with sledges and mounted on deer-back. This race was held on the frozen Kolyma river near the point where it joins the Arctic Ocean. A lorry was driven 2–3 kilometres across the ice towards the middle of the river to mark the turning point. In the distance the faint shapes of other, losing sledgers can be seen.

drove them wild with delight and they became impossible to control. But the herders were also pleased to allow this because it was their last chance to fatten the animals up for the hard winter. Now, all the deer must be found, brought together and driven into the autumn corral where herders will check their weight and condition and decide which ones to send to the village for slaughter. In Soviet terminology, they must 'fulfil their plan' by delivering a specified quantity of meat to the state farm. All those deer which during the summer became weak or were injured must go, as well as many of the males. The best males are kept for breeding, or else castrated for training as working deer. The animals chosen for this training must show strength, intelligence and a cooperative temperament.

In this corral, deer are also vaccinated and the antlers of the breeding males sawn off. By October, they will be rutting and fighting with each other; and males with full antlers may get them tangled up together on a remote mountainside and die. It is the pregnant females who will need their antlers the most during the winter, as they scrape away the snow to feed themselves and their young.

Winter is a season of quiet and calm. With only a few hours of faint light each day, the deer do not move far or fast. Some older herders go trapping animals like squirrel and sable in order to sell the fur; younger ones take the opportunity to spend more time in the village, where they can meet women, watch films and go to dances. The frozen landscape makes movement across the terrain much easier. A ride to the village, which in summer would have taken several days on horseback through swamps, can now be accomplished by reindeer sledge or snowmobile in just a few hours or a day.

Yet the weather is most bitter and, whether herding or travelling, the Eveny feel the cold and take great care to dress appropriately at all times. Outer clothing is made mostly of reindeer fur. Since each individual hair is hollow in the middle, it is extremely heat-retentive. They consider minus 40 degrees Celsius to be quite comfortable. But at minus 50, as they say, 'when you spit, your saliva freezes before it hits the ground, and then you feel really uncomfortable'. Hunters and trappers continue to live in small canvas tents with their wood-burning stoves, but herding brigades often build themselves wooden huts along the winter stretch of their migration route. These are warm and also serve as depots for the equipment which they check and repair during the long winter nights.

There is little activity until late April or May, when the calves are born and the herd is at its largest. From now until midsummer, the workload increases dramatically. The newborn calves and their mothers remain very vulnerable to predators like wolves and bears. During midsummer, when it is light all night, the deer

LEFT: The traditional religion of all Arctic peoples was shamanism. In this vast, lonely and dangerous landscape much of life's fortune, whether in hunting or health, was believed to depend on spirits. The shaman, a kind of spirit-medium, would go onto a trance in order to enable communication between humans and spirits. Shamans enjoyed great respect and considerable power.

RIGHT: Since the 1930s, as part of the Communist reform of society, shamanism has been persecuted and shamans often imprisoned or killed. Under *perestroika*, old shamanic dances are re-enacted as part of a growing pride in indigenous traditions. However, this dance is being performed by a theatre company as part of the festival and it is unlikely that a genuine shamanism can now be revived since the tradition has been largely broken.

are constantly on the move and the herders take it in turns to maintain a 24-hour watch. The night shift ride into the camp early in the morning for a drink of tea with the next shift who are preparing to leave. They pass on vital information about the herd's night-time moves and moods and if there is a shortage of men, they will just snatch a few hours' sleep and go back on duty. Nobody has time for a proper meal. It is during this period that the men are least likely to be able to get to the village to see their families.

Perestroika and the new political conciousness

Just before this period, in March, the Eveny celebrate the advent of spring with a festival. In pre-Soviet times, nomadic clans and families who had lived apart all winter would meet at an agreed place at the spring equinox. Here, they would exchange news and see who had survived the winter. In the absence of any backup from radio, helicopter or shop-bought supplies, this was a serious question. It was also an important time for courtship and marriage. Through physical games like wrestling and reindeer racing, young men would demonstrate their skills and their suitability as husbands to girls and their parents.

Under collectivization, many of these functions became obsolete and the spring festival fell into disuse. However, it was revived in many villages in the early 1980s with the emphasis on the physical games. In the late 1980s, the authorities of the Yakut Republic (which contains many of the USSR's Even communities) brought together the local festivals of each village into one big festival, in which members of the Eveny and other small northern peoples took part. The festival took place in a different location each year, and the various villages would bring their representatives and their champion racing deer over thousands of miles by helicopter. Though this brought together widely scattered branches of the Even people who would otherwise have no chance of contact, the expense was found to be too great; and in 1990 it was decided to end the joint celebration for the time being.

However, the 1990 gathering was more than a folk festival. It also included a meeting of the Yakut Republic's branch of the Association of Northern Peoples, recently founded in Moscow. The Eveny are strongly represented in this branch and the Chairman of the local branch is a well-known Even writer. This meeting received

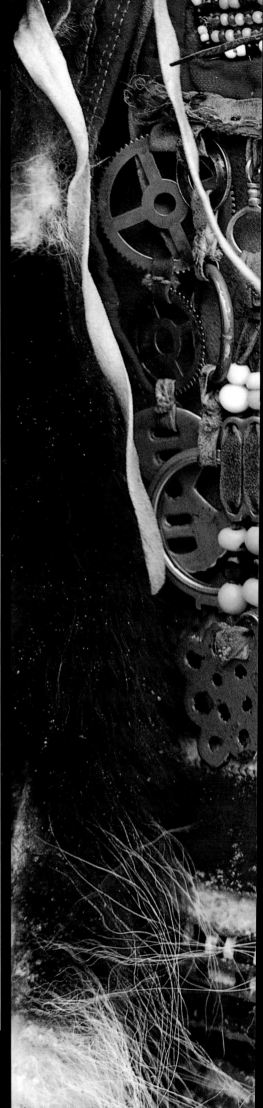

Festival clothing

Spectators at the festival wear their finest clothing. Though in summer Eveny wear manufactured clothing flown into the village shop, in winter they still use clothes made from reindeer fur since this is both warmer and stronger. Even the boots are made of reindeer fur in two layers, the inner one facing inwards and the outer one facing outwards. This climate is an extremely dry one and the snow generally has a dry powdery consistency. Before going indoors, reindeer-fur clothing is thoroughly beaten to shake off any snow and is then hung up to keep it dry. This clothing must not be allowed to get damp. Reindeer fur perishes when taken to another climate.

OPPOSITE TOP: When women lived largely in the herding camps, they sewed fur clothing in the tents during the long summer evenings. Now the clothing is mostly made in centralized workshops in the village, where it is part of an organized programme of women's employment.

LEFT: The elaborate bead ornamentation is not worn every day. It represents hundreds of hours of female labour and is brought out only on special occasions.

OPPOSITE BOTTOM: The silver, in styles of Russian and Yakut origin, is likewise rarely seen and few people now possess any.

wide publicity and gave an important opportunity to speak out on a wide range of problems and anxieties. The discussion of reform is complicated because local people, whether herders or village residents, are closely knit together by kinship and widely implicated in every strand of the old system. It is not simply a question of a Russian administration imposed on a native people, since local people are often dominant in both the administration and the Communist Party.

The festival also included a clear indication of how the Eveny are seeking a clearer sense of their own identity through a return to their cultural roots. In general, Soviet policy towards minority peoples encouraged the development of their language but steered their culture towards pan-Soviet forms and values which were very distant from their hearts. The traditional religion of the Eveny, as of all Arctic peoples, was shamanism. In this vast, lonely and dangerous landscape much of life's fortune, whether in hunting or health, was believed to depend on spirits. The shaman would go into a trance in order to enable communication between humans and spirits. Shamans enjoyed great respect and considerable power and in the early Soviet period were considered to be ringleaders of opposition. From the 1920s onwards, shamanism was often persecuted and shamans imprisoned, exiled or killed. At the festival, a troupe of dancers re-enacted a shamanic dance and were surrounded by a large and curious crowd. Similar displays of shamanic themes are now widespread, though it is unlikely that a genuine shamanism can be revived since the tradition has been largely broken.

Many of those who spoke at the meeting were themselves herders, who appeared in the hall in their reindeer-fur outdoor clothes. Their speeches echoed themes which are already familiar from the Soviet press, which since the early days of *perestroika* has been generally sympathetic to the plight of the northern peoples. Speaker after speaker condemned the environmental degradation of lakes, rivers and pastures. Some of this is caused by mineral workings. But perhaps more serious still

BELOW: The best racing reindeer are transported thousands of kilometres by helicopter to compete in the spring festival.

RIGHT: Snowmobiles make it possible for the Eveny to travel to the village from their camp in just a few hours, but they have only a short range and limited endurance, and are no match for reindeer sledges.

is the contamination caused by the testing of nuclear weapons in the Soviet North from the 1950s until the late 1970s, which is said to have caused a spectacular rise in cancer among the younger generations of northern peoples. Radiation, which is picked up in very high concentrations by lichen, then passes into the reindeer meat which is the staple diet of humans. Speakers were also concerned about the loss of their culture and language. They saw this as directly related to the shortage of young people in traditional occupations such as reindeer herding. To resolve this, they are demanding not only improvements in the material and economic circumstances of herders, but also a reform of schooling. In the first place, they say, a growing proportion of lessons should be held in Even and other native languages, which have recently been losing ground to Russian and Yakut, a dominant regional language. In addition, steps must be taken to provide mobile schooling so that children can at last be educated in the ways of the outside world at the same time as living with their fathers in the camps and learning how to herd reindeer. Above all, they believe that these goals cannot be pursued unless there is radical constitutional reform, which would give them a degree of self-government in their own autonomous territories.

What is the political background to these demands and how realistic are they? Like the rest of the population of the USSR, the native reindeer herders of the Soviet North are undergoing a period of intense change. Their specific situation is widespread throughout the Soviet Arctic but is an unusual one in the USSR as a whole. It amounts to nothing less than considering the restoration of some form of nomadism.

This situation continues to unfold against a new background of *perestroika* nationwide. *Perestroika*, which means 'reconstruction', is envisaged as not only a reconstruction of the economy, but also as a political and social process. In this sense it is ideological, too, involving a fundamental reassessment of the relationship of the state to its citizens and of their mutual obligations. At the heart of this is a process of democratization and decentralization. Ethnic groups, and indeed all Soviet citizens, are thus presented with a situation which arises in history only rarely: they are poised at a decisive moment in the development of the encapsulating state which puts into their hands the possibility of renegotiating their own position in the overall picture.

Peoples like the Eveny are articulate and well-informed about events in the outside world. They are taking ever greater advantage of the channels available for their expression, and trying where possible to force the hand of official policy makers. Local and national papers contain very outspoken pieces by readers and petitions are sent to Mr Gorbachev and other people at the top. Many of their demands

A young girl and a grandmother dressed for outdoors. Eveny are extremely careful to dress adequately and to insulate themselves with many overlapping layers. Though dangerous, life in the tundra and forest can be healthy and older herders are often still active at the age of 90 or 100. However, among the younger generation there are many early deaths from cancer. This is probably caused by the radioactive fallout from nuclear testing in the Soviet Arctic from the 1960s–1970s. Radiation contaminates the lichen, which is grazed by the reindeer and enters the bodies of humans who eat the meat. *Perestroika* now allows the Eveny, like all northern peoples, to campaign vigorously for a ban on testing and for improved medical facilities.

amount to a repudiation of all the early Soviet period stood for, such as collectivization. But they are not simply trying to put the clock back. In tune with the modern world and the evolving situation in the USSR as a whole, they are increasingly turning their attention to political, legal and constitutional demands.

Northern native people are increasingly pointing out the connections between local problems and wider issues of environmentalism and human rights. These connections appear, for example, in the discussion of whether herding communities should be compensated financially for disruption and pollution caused by industrial development, or in the emergence of terms like 'self-government'. There is also a growing awareness that the non-Soviet Arctic, in Scandinavia, Greenland, Canada and Alaska, faces similar difficulties and that there, too, though the circumstances are different and the debate has been open for a long time, there are still no solutions.

At the same time, many of their wants are really specific local reflections of what every Soviet citizen needs throughout the USSR. People are asking for greater control over their own lives and destinies. They want a cleaner environment, in particular a ban on nuclear testing, to which they are especially vulnerable. They want improved health facilities in order to improve their extremely precarious demographic situation. But above all, they want something without which everything else is meaningless: a sense of their own cultural identity and the possibility for herders to have a normal family life again.

This in turn depends on many improvements to the material conditions and morale of herders, but above all on the presence of women and children in the camps. Though the school system has severely damaged family life, the family was never supplanted as the core of the working brigade and it remains central to the herders' view of their own lives. Public pressure is already forcing the administration to abolish boarding schools throughout the native North. But the logistics of returning children to the tents are more uncertain: it is now proposed to place a teacher in each camp of six or seven families. If implemented, this may tilt the focus significantly away from the village in favour of camp life; but it is still far from clear at what age children would have to move on to the village for more advanced education, or where sufficient teachers could be found. This is especially problematic if they are to be expected to teach in the Even language, which very few are yet qualified to do.

Perhaps most troublesome is many people's continuing caution about committing themselves in the long term to a radically new policy which they fear could one day be reversed again. *Perestroika* still seems very precarious and the way ahead very uncertain. People are becoming more and more disheartened about what may be achieved. But the past few years have raised the consciousness of reindeer herders. Even if no one is yet able to propose any clear answers, there is a widespread determination to pose the problem. There is also a recognition that solutions cannot come as they used to, from above. Though their ultimate destiny depends on a battle of the giants several thousand kilometres away in Moscow, the semi-nomadic northern native peoples are keen to seize whatever initiatives they can.

BELOW: As there are no schools in the camps, Even children are educated in the village, living in boarding school if they have no close relatives in the village to care for them. This has been a major factor in the breakdown of family life. Teaching, moreover, is largely in Russian with the result that their native language and culture are becoming alien to them. The quote from Lenin in this picture reads, 'Young people must study . . . study Communism'.

CONTRIBUTORS

EDITOR/PHOTOGRAPHER

Peter Carmichael, originator and co-producer of the television series which this book accompanies, is a photographer and writer who has been documenting the lives of nomadic peoples worldwide for the last twenty years. He was born in Kenya and has travelled throughout Africa, the Middle East and Far East, including China and Tibet. His books include *A World of Islands*, which deals with the island peoples of the South West Pacific, *The Royal Kingdom of Saudi Arabia*, *Oman* and *China*. He has also worked on assignment for *National Geographic* (Washington) and *Geo* (Germany).

WRITERS

Dr André Singer has a doctorate in social anthropology from Oxford University and is Professor of Anthropology at the University of Southern California. Former Series Editor of the award-winning Granada Television series *Disappearing World*, he is a distinguished documentary film-maker and is currently Editor for Development in documentary features at the BBC. His previous books include *Guardians of the North West Frontier* and *Lords of the Khyber* (both on the Pathans of Afghanistan) and *Battle for the Planet* (an environmental book).

Diana Stone graduated from the School of Oriental and African Studies, University of London, with a first class honours degree in social anthropology. She is currently involved in field work in Mauritania and is preparing a Ph.D thesis on the Moors and Islam. She has travelled extensively in Mauritania and speaks Hassaniyya.

Dr J. Terrence McCabe is Assistant Professor of Anthropology and Professional Staff, Institute of Behavioral Sciences, at the University of Colorado, USA. He began field work with the Turkana in 1980 as part of his dissertation research and has lived among the Turkana people for four and a half years. His previous publications include *South Turkana Pastoralism: Coping with an Unpredictably Varying Environment* (with Rada Dyson-Hudson) and numerous articles. He received a Ph.D in 1985 from the State University of New York at Binghamton.

Steven Seidenberg was awarded degrees in Chinese Studies from the University of Illinois and the University of London before beginning the postgraduate study of social anthropolgy at Oxford University in 1975. Since leaving Oxford University in 1983, he has divided his time between documentary film-making and writing. He has made three films on China: *Shifting Sands* (1986), *Cold Spring, Morning Sun* (1988) and *The Fragrant Smoke* (1989).

Dr Piers Vitebsky is a social anthropologist and Head of Social Sciences at the Scott Polar Research Institute in the University of Cambridge. He has carried out many years' field work in tribal India, Sri Lanka and Arctic Siberia and speaks several local languages. His book *Dialogues with the dead: the discussion of mortality, loss and continuity among the Sora of central India* will be published by Cambridge University Press in 1992. Recently he has been working with semi-nomadic reindeer herders north of Yakutsk in the Soviet Union.

FURTHER READING

Very little is available for the general reader on any of the four groups covered in this book, but the following titles and articles may be of interest.

THE MOORS OF MAURITANIA
Belvaude, C. *La Mauritanie* (Lamartin, 1989)
Norris, H.T. *Shinquiti Folk Literature and Song* (Clarendon Press, 1968, op)
Park, Mungo *Travels into the Interior of Africa* (Eland, 1983)

THE TURKANA OF KENYA
Amin, M. *The Cradle of Mankind* (The Overlook Press, Woodstock, New York, 1983)
Brown, M. *Where Giants Trod: The Saga of Kenya's Desert Lake* (Quiller Press Ltd, 1990)
Fratkin, E. 'Two Lives for the Ariaal', *Natural History Magazine* (1989)
Dyson-Hudson, N. 'Turkana' in *Primitive Worlds: People Lost in Time* (National Geographic Society, 1973)
McCabe, J.T. and **Ellis, J.E.** 'Beating the Odds in Arid Africa' *Natural History*, Vol. 96, #1, pp. 33–41. Reprinted in *Conformity and Conflict*, Spreadley and McCurdy eds. Scott, Foresman/Little Brown Publications in Higher Education 1987

THE HORSEMEN OF MONGOLIA
Bawden, C.R. *The Modern History of Mongolia* (Weidenfeld and Nicholson, 1968, new edition 1989)
Jagchid, S. and **Hyer, P.** *Mongolia's Culture and Society* (Dawson, Folkstone, 1979)
Montagu, I. *Land of the Blue Sky* (Dobson, 1956)
Morgan, D. *The Mongols* (Blackwell, 1986)
Onan, U. *My Childhood in Mongolia* (O.U.P., 1972)

THE REINDEER HERDERS OF SIBERIA
Levin, M.G. and **Vasil'yev, B.A.** 'The Evens' in M.G. Levin and L.P. Potapov, eds. *The Peoples of Siberia* (Chicago University Press, 1964)
Vitebsky, P. 'Centralised decentralisation: the ethnography of remote reindeer herders under *perestroika*', *Cahiers du monde russe et soviétique*, XXXI(2–3), 1990, pp. 307–316
Vitebsky, P. '*Perestroika* among the reindeer herders of Siberia', *Geographical Magazine*, LXI:6, June 1989, pp. 22–5
Vitebsky, P. 'Reindeer herders of northern Yakutia: a report from the field', *Polar Record* 24 (154), July 1989, pp. 213–8
Vitebsky, P. 'The crisis in Siberian reindeer herding today: a technical or a social problem?' in Alan Wood and Walter Joyce, eds, *Siberia in the twentieth century: society and economic development* (Longman, to be published in 1992)

INDEX

ACKNOWLEDGEMENTS

Any project the size of NOMADS, which consists of a book and four documentary films, can never be the work of one person. Such a mammoth undertaking required a dedicated team of professionals to bring it to completion. In all the project has taken three years and it is to this team of people, both here in London and on location, that I would like to convey my profound gratitude, for without their assistance and advice, NOMADS would have been shelved long ago.

NOMADS is also my small way of saying thank you to all those nomadic families who have gone out of their way to help me so much over the past 25 years. Being with them and experiencing their day-to-day lives was a privilege and gave a purpose to my life the like of which I can never repay.

This project would never have got off the ground had it not been for Gérard de la Vallée Poussin, Peter Doran and Derek Roy. Not only are they personal friends but it was they who believed in NOMADS from the outset and as a result underwrote the bulk of the pre-production funding. At the same time, I would like to convey my sincere thanks to Colin Campbell who has been my support throughout and introduced ITEL (the marketing distribution company for the documentaries) and Malone Gill who were the production company. Claire Rawcliffe and David Capey were also kind enough to guide me through a very raw patch in the early days.

In addition, I would like to thank André Singer for his support and advice over the last two years, and the anthropologists – Piers Vitebsky, Terry McCabe, Diana Stone and Margaret Willson – whose expertise and familiarity with their respective nomadic groups provided the entrée so vital to the nature of this project. They, together with Steve Seidenberg, collectively made this book possible. Last, yet by no means least, I would like to thank Sarah Hoggett (my editor at Collins & Brown) who, together with Mark Collins and Gabrielle Townsend, provided unfailing support from the start.

I would also like to acknowledge the following people whose assistance gave birth to NOMADS: Nadia Warner; John Paul Rathbone; Derek and Angela Bayes; John Miller; Tim Bailey; Sarah Errington; Marion van Offelen; Roderick Hulsbergen; Sue White; Amina Mins; Baqer Moin; Professor E.A. Gellner; Professor Philip Salzman; Professor Gunnar Holland; Dr Richard Tapper; Dr Shirin Akiner, Dr Paul Baxter, and Dr Paul Henley.

ON LOCATION
Kenya Bethwell Kiplagat; J.B. Nabali; Patrick Wangira; Jean Hartley; Jill Curtis; Mike Pool; Tim and Anthea Barton; Mary and Gerald Nevill.
Mauritania Didi Ould Soueydi; Tijani Ould Kerim; Abdallahi Ould Mohamed; Medullah Ould Bollah.
Soviet Union Pavel Tsarvulanov and Aleksey Drogaitsev of Start Corporation; Topolino Sovkhoz.
China Naranhuar; Li Shou Hua; Zhai Wen Li; Meng Xianjun; China Film Co-Production Corporation; Xu Chunging; Li Jian; Jia Yung Ann

Finally, I would like to dedicate NOMADS to my wife Sharon, who, together with my mother, has supported and encouraged my work in this project from the start. How she puts up with my lifestyle I will never know; but it is her understanding and patience that has often given me the will to continue when times have been tough.